School Review
and Inspection

The Management and Leadership in Education Series

Series Editor: Howard Green

Competences for School Managers Derek Esp
Educational Values for School Leadership Sylvia West
Essential School Leadership Gary Holmes
School Review and Inspection David Woods and Susan Orlik

School Review
and Inspection

David Woods and
Susan Orlik

KOGAN
PAGE

London • Philadelphia

Kogan Page Limited
120 Pentonville Road
London N1 9JN

© David Woods and Susan Orlik, 1994

British Library Cataloguing in Publication Data

A CIP record for this book is available from the British Library.

ISBN 0 7494 0986 X

Typeset by Saxon Graphics Ltd, Derby
Printed and bound in Great Britain by
Biddles Ltd, Guildford and King's Lynn.

Contents

Series Editor's Foreword *Howard Green*   7
Acknowledgements   9
Introduction   11

1 **A Concern for Quality and School Improvement**   13

2 **The Process of Inspection**   22
    The Framework for Inspection   23
    The record of evidence   24
    Inspection methodology   25
    The inspection report   25
    Schools considered to require special measures   26
    The Registered Inspector   27
    Inspection teams   29
    Lay inspectors   30
    Governing bodies   31
    Headteachers and staff   33
    Pupils   35
    Parents   36

3 **Reviewing your own School**   39
    The processes   39
    The cycle   40
    The link to external inspection   41
    The methodology   41
    The particular challenges of reviewing your own school   49

4 **Standards and Quality Achieved** **52**
Analysis of achievement data 54
Value added 56
Lesson observation 58
Pupils' work 61
Profiles/records of achievement 62
Two strategies 62

5 **Quality of Teaching and of Learning** **69**
Methods of internal review 71
Review of evidence and criteria 75

6 **The Curriculum** **85**
Content, organization and planning 85
Cross-curricular themes, skills and dimensions 89
Equality of opportunity 92
Provision for pupils with Special Educational Needs 94
Personal and social education 96
The pre-vocational curriculum 97
Extra-curricular activities 98
Methods of reviewing curriculum quality and range 99

7 **Pupils' Personal Development and Behaviour** **109**
A method of internal review (PSMSCD) 110
Structuring an internal review 114
Structuring an internal review of behaviour and discipline 115
Structuring an internal review of attendance 117

8 **Management, Administration and Efficiency** **124**
Methods of internal review 125
Structuring an internal review (MAE) 125
Review of evidence and criteria 132

Postscript **145**
Bibliography **152**
Index **153**

Series Editor's Foreword

The government's educational reforms have created an unprecedented rate of change in schools. They have also raised fundamental questions about the purposes of education and the nature of school management and leadership. Similar changes are occurring in other educational systems throughout the world.

In this context there is an urgent need for all of us with an interest in education to step back and reflect on recent educational reforms, to reaffirm old truths and successful practice where appropriate, to sift out and implement the best of new ideas, modifying or abandoning those which are a distraction from the central purpose of schools: to ensure that an education of high quality is a guaranteed opportunity for *all* our children and young people.

This series has been planned to satisfy the demand for short, readable books for busy people and with a focus on single issues at the forefront of school management and leadership. They are written by reflective practitioners who are either working in schools or directly with those who do. The series celebrates the ideals, skills and experience of professionals in education who want to see further improvements in our schools.

Both of this book's authors are Registered Inspectors. Susan Orlik has recent experience of both senior management in schools and advisory work. She is currently the Headteacher of Langley School, a comprehensive in Solihull. David Woods is Head of the Schools Advisory Service and an accredited OFSTED trainer for one of the largest local education authorities in England and Wales. The authors write about a fundamental task of management: on-going school review and about a most important government reform: the new approach to school inspection which is organized by the Office for Standards in Education (OFSTED).

It was in 1977 that the former Inner London Education Authority published the little buff booklet *Keeping the School under Review* with the sub-title 'a method of self-assessment for schools'. The booklet was a seminal publication because it became the inspiration for similar school review processes in many local education authorities throughout the UK. These processes have now been integrated into the 'audit' stage of school development planning which attempts to draw together all aspects of school management and leadership. Review or audit precedes planning of the curriculum, staffing and finance which are then followed by target-setting and implementation. Then there is further review of the outcomes and so the planning cycle repeats itself.

It is the aim of the government that all state-maintained primary and secondary schools will be inspected once every four years according to the procedures now established by OFSTED. The inspection report will be a public document available to the school, its governors and parents and the media. It represents the public accountability of the education service and is based on very explicit criteria. Schools need to know about and be prepared for their OFSTED inspection. Ideally the inspection should be integrated as a natural dimension of on-going school review.

This timely addition to the 'Management and Leadership in Education' series does just that – it informs readers about the OFSTED inspection process and places it in the wider context of school review as part of the development planning process.

Howard Green
Eggbuckland

Acknowledgements

It is with real gratitude that we want to record our thanks to Judith Hicks, Head of the Inspection Unit, University of Birmingham, who read the manuscript with her customary incisiveness and generous help. Any errors which remain are ours alone.

We would also like to thank all those teachers with whom we work, and have worked. Such a book is naturally the product of the skills and dedication of those teachers who have always sought to improve their practice and that of their schools. It is the greatest privilege to have worked, and to work, with these teachers.

Finally, we would like to thank Leri Woods and Michael Orlik, who have corrected and criticized the proofs, as well as enduring cheerfully this collaborative venture. Since acknowledgement of their support is insufficient, we would ask them to accept this dedication instead.

SUSAN ORLIK
DAVID WOODS

Introduction

The purpose of inspection as described by the *Handbook for the Inspection of Schools* (HMI, 1992) is 'to identify strengths and weaknesses in schools so that they may improve the quality of education offered and raise the standards achieved by their pupils'. It is a form of quality assurance carried out by an agency external to the school, using an agreed schedule, focused on appropriate evidence and evaluation criteria and informed by quantitative indicators. An inspection report is a judgement of where a school is in terms of effectiveness at a given point of time.

The purpose of school review is to establish and use a continuous process of internal monitoring and evaluation to develop the means of school improvement. The evaluation criteria in the Framework for Inspection can be used as a basis for this, along with other agreed criteria. The principles underpinning school review include the collection of evidence against set criteria, seeking both quantitative and qualitative information, identifying performance measures and making appropriate judgements which will help set targets for the further development of school effectiveness.

This book seeks to provide schools and the educational community generally with a practical guide to school inspection within the context of continuous school review. It is the view of the authors that inspection will be managed successfully where it is seen as a complementary process to continuous school review and improvement. Both OFSTED inspections and school reviews are concerned with monitoring and evaluation. School review offers a process of self-supported evaluation, a method of 'internal' inspection and review of school effectiveness. OFSTED inspections are an external judgement on school effectiveness, which ideally seeks to validate the internal methods and outcomes of school review, and make a judgement on the quality of education offered and standards achieved.

Chapter 1 reviews some of the criteria and processes for the development of quality and school improvement in terms of national and international research which can be used to underpin the individual school's review process. Chapter 2 concentrates on the process of inspection, as introduced in the Education (Schools) Act of 1992, and the provision of a *Handbook for the Inspection of Schools* (rewritten in August 1993) with a view to providing guidance on the Framework for Inspection itself, inspection methodology and the roles of the key stakeholders in the process, such as the Registered Inspector, the inspection team, the governing body, headteachers and staff, pupils and parents. Chapter 3 gives practical guidance on how to review your own school, which includes the processes, cycle and methodologies of review and the link to OFSTED inspections. Chapters 4-8 deal in depth with major aspects of the inspection schedule itself: standards and quality achieved; quality of teaching and learning; the curriculum, including equality of opportunity and provision for pupils with Special Educational Needs; pupils' personal development and behaviour; and efficiency, management and administration. They also give practical help and guidance in the form of checklists, strategies and methodologies in the review of each aspect. At the end of each of these chapters there is a table describing what the school can do for internal review (both whole-school and curriculum areas) and what the inspectors can do, together with appropriate Inspection Framework references. The Postscript offers a comprehensive checklist for heads, teachers and governors to consider for school review and preparation for inspection.

Chapter 1

A Concern for Quality and School Improvement

The mission statements and published aims of all schools demonstrate their responsibility for facilitating the development of every pupil as effectively as possible. Further, most schools demonstrate a concern for quality and improvement in the way that they attempt to translate aims into development plans and to measure their performance against predetermined success criteria and performance indicators. This chapter reviews some of the criteria and processes for school improvement in the context of inspections every four years. A school that is familiar with the processes behind quality development and school improvement will be much better placed to assimilate an inspection audit into its own system of review. To help you evaluate your own school's improvement strategies, it may be useful first to look further at research that has been carried out into what makes an effective school.

There is a considerable amount of evidence, particularly from research done over the last 15 years, that individual schools can make a significant difference to pupil progress and that some schools are more effective than others in helping pupils to progress, both in social and academic terms. However, while it used to be assumed that schools with good examination results and assessment outcomes were also the schools with good attendance rates, low levels of pupil misbehaviour and a high quality of relationships, it is now more evident that schools good in one area may not be as good at promoting pupil growth in other areas. School effectiveness may vary across a range of indicators and may involve decisions as to where a school places its maximum efforts to excel in. Another variable to consider in school effectiveness is how far schools are differentially effective for individual pupils and groups of pupils in terms of gender, ability, ethnicity and social circumstance. There is also emerging evidence about the variations between parts of the school in their effectiveness. In secondary schools, there can be big differences between departments judged by assessment outcomes, and in 'effective' schools there will be less satisfactory teaching and learning in some areas; in 'ineffective' schools there will be good teaching in some areas. A similar imbalance will be present in primary schools, whatever the overall picture, with variations in the education experiences of pupils due to teaching standards in particular classes. School effectiveness also varies over time, as schools are dynamic institutions and schools can move from being ineffective to effective and vice versa in as little as two or three years. Therefore, in order to measure themselves on an effectiveness scale, schools need to review their provision against four general questions, and you may wish to apply these to your own school.

- Are schools effective in every area – academic, social, caring?
- Are schools effective for all individual pupils and groups of pupils?
- Are different parts of the school more effective than others in terms of teaching and learning? Are there significant differences in subjects and classes?
- How do effective schools sustain effectiveness and ineffective schools begin to improve?

Clearly, it is also important to come to a consensus of what is an effective school, and much of the research has identified certain internal conditions as typical in schools that achieve a higher level of outcomes for their pupils, although there is less consensus on what *process* factors will provide these outcomes.

One of the first major studies of school effectiveness in Britain was written by Rutter *et al* in 1979, comparing the effects of ten secondary schools in inner London. They identified the key factors in school effectiveness as:

- school values, expectations and standards;
- good classroom management;
- teacher action in lessons and high expectations;
- teachers as positive role models;

- positive feedback and treatment of pupils;
- good working conditions for pupils and teachers;
- pupils given responsibility;
- pupils' experience of success and achievement;
- shared staff and pupil activities.

Together, these factors made up an 'ethos' or 'culture' which enabled schools to improve.

In *Secondary Schools: An Appraisal by HMI* (1988) HMI set out the following 12 criteria for effectiveness distilled from the findings of inspections of nearly 200 secondary schools, which they had found applied to the best schools:

- good leadership – by heads, deputies, departmental and pastoral staff;
- clear aims and associated objectives translated into classroom practice, implemented and monitored;
- emphasis on high academic standards, encouraging all pupils to achieve to their potential;
- a relevant, but orderly and firm, classroom atmosphere;
- good relationships with pupils, who were encouraged to express views, understood the purposes of lessons and were strongly motivated;
- a coherent curriculum, well-planned and implemented, and serving the needs of pupils;
- concern for pupils' development as individuals in society, with a commitment by staff to their personal and social development, and effective guidance;
- well-qualified staff, with experience and expertise – skilfully deployed and in receipt of appropriate development and training;
- suitable and respected working accommodation with appropriate specialist rooms and an aesthetically stimulating environment;
- effectively deployed and managed material resources;
- good relationships with community, parents and governors;
- the capacity to manage change, solve problems and develop organically.

Smith and Tomlinson's study of multi-racial comprehensive schools (1989) identified considerable differences between schools in terms of effectiveness and identified certain conditions as being typical of successful schools:

- leadership and management in school by the headteacher and heads of department;
- teacher involvement in decision making (curriculum, methods, organization, use of resources and whole-school policies);
- a climate of respect (between teachers, pupils–pupils, pupils–teachers, teachers–parents etc) and respect for other cultures;
- positive feedback to and treatment of pupils.

In the primary phase, research done by Mortimore *et al* (1988) on key factors of effectiveness in junior schools listed twelve factors which accounted for differential effectiveness between schools:

- purposeful leadership of the staff by the headteacher;
- the involvement of the deputy head;
- the involvement of teachers in planning, development and decision making;
- consistency among teachers;
- structured learning sessions;
- intellectually challenging teaching;
- work-centred environment;
- limited focus within lessons;
- maximum communication between teacher and pupils;
- record-keeping linked to planning and assessment;
- parental involvement with the life of the school;
- a positive climate.

In another study of education of young children in early years education (Tizard *et al*, 1988) particular factors associated with attainment and progress in infant schools were:

- pre-school attainments;
- mother's level of education;
- teacher's expectations (consistently too low);
- parent–teacher co-operation.

International research into school effectiveness has also contributed considerably to the debate and organizational characteristics of effective schools and these are remarkably similar from country to country, usually including the following elements:

- a specifically directed system for monitoring performance and achievement;
- a curriculum which is clearly defined and co-ordinated;
- leadership – a headteacher who can combine setting goals and motivating staff to achieve them, while making sure that staff are involved in the process of decision-making;
- staff development programmes which involve a commitment to long-term growth;
- maximizing learning time, and purposeful and challenging teaching, together with appropriate use of homework;
- recognition for pupil success across a wide range of academic, social, sporting and cultural areas;
- parental and community involvement.

In England and Wales, the 1988 Education Reform Act and the arrival of Local Management of Schools accentuated the need for schools to establish performance indicators and systems of evaluation, and to monitor operations at all levels of schooling – institutional, subject and process. The purpose of performance indicators is to raise questions, possibly prompting a school to probe more deeply and to provide information from a variety of evidence about what is happening or what has taken place in a school. The use of these indicators makes a big contribution to the question every school needs to ask about itself: 'Where are we now?' In 1989 the DES (as it then was) published a list of factors relevant to performance indicators which referred to input considerations such as pupil intake, resources and background, and process indicators such as staff, teacher deployment, curriculum arrangements, wider educational practices, organization and relationships, and outcome indicators such as performance in internal activities, attendance, lateness, behaviour, participation in sporting, social and cultural activities, and academic attainment.

The challenge for schools is to develop and use their own indicators of quality and effectiveness so that they can evaluate strengths and weaknesses, and set and monitor targets for the future. John Gray, of Sheffield University, suggests (1990) that these should be limited to monitoring three central aspects of a school's performance:

- *academic progress:* what proportion of pupils have made above-average levels of progress over the relevant time period?

- *pupil satisfaction*: what proportion of pupils in the school are satisfied with the education they are receiving?
- *pupil–teacher relationships*: what proportion of pupils in the school have a good or 'vital' relationship with one or more teachers?

The process of school development planning helps to manage this process of innovation, and to change and ultimately improve the quality of teaching and learning through posing four basic questions:

- where is the school now?
- what changes are needed?
- how should these changes be managed over time?
- how will the school know whether it has been successful?

Four main processes are used in the development planning cycle:

- audit – reviewing strategy and values;
- construction – turning priorities into targets;
- implementation – implementing those targets;
- evaluation – checking the success of implementation.

The 1992 Education (Schools) Act has now pushed the process one step further by legislating for the external inspection of every school once every four years, a form of quality control of school development and improvement. The *Handbook for the Inspection of Schools* (of which the Framework for Inspection forms Part 2) was written by HMI (1992, 2nd ed. 1993) for this purpose and the functions of inspection set out in the Act are to report on:

- 'the educational standards achieved in those schools';
- 'the quality of education provided by schools';
- 'whether the financial resources made available to those schools are managed efficiently';
- 'the spiritual, moral, social and cultural development of pupils at those schools' (P4).

Although schools may be very aware from the research of the key factors and organizational characteristics of effective schools, and equally aware of performance indicators, evaluation criteria and evidence used to judge that effectiveness through inspection and review, they may be less certain of the *process* factors that can help a school to improve over time. Real school improvement is nothing less than the transformation of the culture of a school so that it can improve its capacity to sustain and manage educational change. Many schools will have experimented with change processes, whether in curriculum, management, or teaching and learning styles, and some will have tried full-scale review checklists and self-evaluation systems such as the guidelines for review and internal development in schools (GRIDS). In some cases these will have been innovations which may not have taken root because attempts have been made to graft them on to an unchanged culture. The professional development of teachers may have been superficial and partial rather than at the heart of long-term professional growth. It is essential, therefore, that schools identify and write down their own process characteristics that will underpin their school improvement.

The *process* characteristics of effective schools, gathered from research evidence, would seem to be:

– a guiding and shared value system with a consensus on aims, goals, expectations, rules and social order;
– collaborative planning and collegial relationships where there are agreed whole-school policies with shared decision-making to increase commitment;
– a sense of community in the school with intense interaction and communication at all levels, and high-quality relationships;
– a capacity to stimulate, absorb and manage change with appropriate leadership at both horizontal and vertical levels, supported by frequent evaluation to further improve performance (see Figure 1.1).

Such schools are reflective, 'thinking' schools constantly aware, through a process of dynamic development-planning, of where they are and where they would like to get to, and having the means, through their open culture, of implementing and sustaining change and improvement. They will have established success criteria for school effectiveness which will be concerned with process indicators, and suggest how practice can be improved and what are the expectations for achievement. You might find it helpful to consider the following examples:

– teachers make good and consistent use of praise and rewards;
– teachers hold high expectations of all pupils;
– all teachers are involved in curriculum planning and the development of school policies;

- all pupil achievements are recorded and the recorded information is used by teachers;
- time is set aside for giving pupils feedback about their work;
- the school has a clear system for reviewing its own policies and practices.

Improvement programmes in schools have to be integral to the life of the school, and spring from an enduring concern for quality and improvement. These improvements will be validated from time to time by external agencies such as LEAs and through OFSTED inspections. Change will involve both the structure and organization of the school and the informal cultural world of staff relationships, expectations and feelings, and the change process will be long-term, involving a cycle of review, improvement and evaluation. What is vital is that the school develops itself as a professional community involving teachers at every level in a continual process of collective self-review, based upon an analysis of the aims, goals and values of the institution itself. If the school is able to do this, then it will be able to manage inspection effectively as a complementary process to real school improvement.

Figure 1.1 *Characteristics of the effective school*

High expectations and challenging teaching, together with the recognition of achievement across a wide range of areas

A sense of community, and shared decision-making and collaborative planning to improve commitment

An orderly, safe and corporate community with a shared social order, which gives structure for pupils' and teachers' activities

A SHARED SCHOOL CULTURE AND CLIMATE

Curriculum change and development at all levels of the school, impacting on the quality and teaching of learning

Accountability to external review and inspection, with the use of indicators and evidence as measures

Professional development with a commitment to long-term personal and intellectual growth and development

Internal monitoring and evaluating systems of the school's policies and practices with established success criteria

Chapter 2
The Process of Inspection

Having looked at the criteria and processes of school improvement, the purpose of this chapter is to provide you with guidance on the process of external inspection which should complement your strategies for school self-review and improvement. There have always been national and local inspectors of schools, but the major differences of the new inspections are: the regular four-year cycle, the public nature of the content of inspection and increased public accountability.

Section 9 of the Education (Schools) Act 1992 makes provision for the inspection of all nursery, county, voluntary and special schools maintained by LEAs, grant maintained schools, non-maintained special schools, city technical colleges, and independent schools approved by the Secretary of State under the 1981 Act as suitable for children for whom statements of special needs are maintained by the LEA. Inspection will be part of a regular cycle, which will take place on a four-yearly basis.

The *purpose* of inspection as defined by the Framework for Inspection is 'to identify strengths and weaknesses in schools in order that they may improve the quality of education offered and raise the standards achieved by their pupils. Particular attention is to be paid to pupils' standards of achievement which are better or worse in any subject than the average for their age group, and to the reasons for such differences'. The *function* of inspection, as set out in the Act, was described above in Chapter 1, page 18.

Inspections will be undertaken by teams of 'independent' inspectors trained in the Framework for Inspection developed on behalf of Her Majesty's Chief Inspectors of Schools (HMCI), which forms a basis for ensuring the quality and reliability of inspections, which must be founded upon appropriate evidence and evaluation criteria, and informed by quantitative indicators. Each inspection team will consist of a Registered Inspector, team members and a lay inspector, all of whom must have been trained and accredited by OFSTED for the appropriate phase and type of school.

The minimum number of inspector days in schools of various types and sizes is prescribed in the Framework for Inspection, and ranges from 5 inspector days in the smallest nursery school to 57 days in the largest secondary school.

The Framework for Inspection

This Framework (Part 2 of the *Handbook*) sets out the content, evaluation criteria and the evidence base of the inspection, and this provides a consistent framework for all schools and gives them a secure foundation on which to base internal school reviews as well as to prepare for inspection. The key areas of the school's work that will be reported on are:

- standards of achievement;
- quality of learning;
- efficiency of the school;
- pupils' personal development and behaviour.

Factors contributing to these findings are described as:

- quality of teaching;
- assessment, recording and reporting;
- quality and range of the curriculum, including equality of opportunity (curriculum organization and planning);
- provision for pupils with special educational needs;
- management and administration;
- resources and their management;
- pupils' welfare and guidance;
- links with parents, agencies and other institutions.

Subjects of the curriculum and other curricular provisions will be inspected according to:

- standards of achievement;
- quality of learning;

- quality of teaching;
- assessment, recording and reporting;
- curriculum content: subject quality and range; equality of opportunities;
- provision for pupils with special educational needs;
- management and administration;
- resources and their management.

The record of evidence

The Registered Inspectors will need to maintain a record of the evidence base during the inspection to ensure that the evidence constitutes a sufficient and valid sample of the work of the school. The record of evidence is a summary of the evidence gathered during the inspection process, and it assists the inspection team in making clear judgements and provides HMCI with formal returns of evidence on which the inspection findings are based. It will consist of the following:

- quantitative data provided by the school;
- lesson observations and grades;
- discussions with members of staff;
- discussions with pupils;
- subject/aspect summary sheets;
- pupils' written and other work;
- other evidence, including observation of general pupil abilities and school meetings.

In the evaluation of the record of evidence there will be included at the end of each section a series of statements setting out the principal judgements the inspectors have to make. The statements are directly related to the evaluation criteria, relevant to each section, which are used as the basis for making judgements. An example of such a statement is:

Accommodation (Framework numbering 7.6.3)
The use of accommodation (in terms of its effect on the quality of teaching and learning):

very effective   x x x x x x x   very ineffective

For each section of the Framework the inspectors should indicate where the judgements they have made lie along the seven-point scale.

Inspection methodology

Lesson observation must constitute the major form of evidence and the sample of lessons and classes inspected must constitute an adequate cross-section of the work of the school. Lesson observations will be recorded on a standard OFSTED pro forma for inclusion in the record of inspection evidence. There is another pro forma for observation of work other than in lessons, such as registration periods, assemblies and extra-curricular activities. The *Handbook for the Inspection of Schools* (Part 3) offers some guidelines in planning the sample of work, which state that in the majority of schools, the size of the sample of lessons observed should normally be between 10 per cent and 20 per cent of the total number of lessons taught during the period of inspection. They suggest that in primary and small secondary schools the sample would need to be over 20 per cent, and in very large secondary schools it may be smaller than 10 per cent, but in no circumstances should it be less than 7 per cent.

Pupils' earlier, recent and current work provides another source of evidence, some of which will be seen during the observation of lessons, but others will result from a systematic sampling of work across the age and ability ranges within the school. Where possible, the inspection team will discuss aspects of the work examined with the pupils who produced it. Other pupil activities will also be observed during the working day, together with extra-curricular activities, and discussions with pupils will be ongoing throughout the inspection.

Oral evidence will be sought from the headteacher, senior management staff, heads of department/post-holders and other middle managers, a sample of other staff and governors, parents and representatives of the community, if available. Where appropriate, inspectors will attend meetings of staff and governors, and those involving the wider community.

The new *Handbook* (1993) contains a code of conduct for inspectors which sets out the basic principles which should govern the conduct of inspectors under the Statutory Framework for the Inspection of Schools.

The inspection report

The required structure of the report is set out at the beginning of Part 2 of the Framework for Inspection and consists of:

- basic information about the school;
- intake of pupils and the area served by the school;
- school data and indications;
- record of the evidence;
- date of the inspection;
- main findings – standards, quality, efficiency and ethos;
- key issues to be addressed.

The rest of the report will be written up under the schedule headings (Part A) of Standards and Quality Achieved, the Efficiency of the School and the Pupils' Personal Development and Behaviour and Factors Contributing to these Findings and Subjects of the Curriculum (Part B).

In reaching a judgement about the overall quality of the school, the Registered Inspectors will need to:

- 'take into account the judgements which have been made on each aspect of the school';
- 'take into account the strength of available evidence for each separate evaluation';
- 'ensure that full weight is given to standards and quality, efficiency and the quality of the school as a community to factors contributing to the outcomes';
- 'take particular note of the corporate judgements of the team'.

The Registered Inspector is responsible for the preparation and issue of the Report and Summary for Parents within 35 working days of the start of the inspection, as specified in the contract with HMCI. The complete report and summary must be sent to the governors or whoever is the appropriate authority, OFSTED and the LEA (if an LEA school) or the Secretary of State (if a GM (grant-maintained) school).

Schools considered to require special measures

Where the Registered Inspector is of the opinion that the school is failing, or is likely to fail, to give the pupils an acceptable standard of education, he or she is under a statutory duty to express that opinion in the report. The criteria to be used in determining whether a school may require special measures are specified in the Framework (Section 1). They are in brief:

- underachievement among the majority of pupils; poor examination results and levels of attainment;
- regular disruptive behaviour and high levels of truancy;
- demoralization and disenchantment among staff; a high proportion of unsatisfactory teaching; low expectations; poor relationships with pupils;
- ineffectiveness of the headteacher and/or senior management; extensive friction between staff and senior management.

The presence of one of these characteristics would not necessarily mean that the school was at risk, and an important consideration would be the inspector's view of the direction in which the school was moving. Some schools may be deteriorating; others may be improving.

HMCI must agree or disagree with the Registered Inspector's opinion and the Registered Inspector must state in the report whether HMCI agrees or disagrees. When HMCI agrees with that opinion, the provisions of the Act in relation to special measures are triggered. These measures state that:

- the appropriate authority must make an action plan;
- the implementation of those action plans must be monitored;
- in the case of a county or voluntary school, the LEA has the power to appoint additional governors and to supervise the delegation of the school's budget;
- the Secretary of State, where he judges it appropriate, may transfer the responsibility for conducting the school to an Education Association, a corporate body set up by and responsible to the Secretary of State.

In order to understand the inspection process fully, it is important to examine this from the standpoint of the main stakeholders – the Registered Inspector, the inspection team, the governing body, headteachers and staff, and pupils and parents.

The Registered Inspector

Registered Inspectors will be at the heart of the system of inspection and OFSTED will award contracts to inspect schools to them, or the contractors they work for. They must have satisfactorily completed an appropriate course of training organized or approved by HMCI, part of which will involve participation in an institutional inspection. In responding to the inspection specification set out by HMCI, the Registered Inspector will need to demonstrate that the inspection will be carried out by a team of inspectors which is sufficient and competent to conduct the inspection as set out under the schedule, that all members are trained, and that the team complies with the Act.

During the inspection, the Registered Inspector should plan the assignments and deployment of team members to ensure coverage of the full range of topics in the schedule, and consultation with the school before the inspection will establish agreed times for the availability of staff, pupils and their work. As soon as the Registered Inspectors begin to conduct inspections, OFSTED will be monitoring their work in order to keep the standard of inspections and reports under review. This will be done through the checking of reports and summaries, and visits by HMI to observe the Registered Inspector at work.

After the inspection, the Framework requires the Registered Inspector to offer to discuss the main findings of the inspection with both the headteacher and members of the senior management team, and separately with the governing body in the presence of the head. This should be done as soon as possible after the end of the inspection and before the report is issued. However, unless there are serious factual inaccuracies which have a bearing on the main findings, there can be no modification or negotiation of the judgements to be included in the report.

Registered Inspectors are required to demonstrate that their judgements are:

secure   – based on substantial evidence and specified quantitative indicators.

first-hand   – based largely on direct observation of pupils' and teachers' work.

reliable   – consistent with evaluation criteria set out in the Framework.

valid   – reflect the standards actually achieved.

comprehensive – cover all aspects of the school set out in the Framework.

corporate   – conclusions reflect the collective view of the inspection team.

Checklist of the Registered Inspector's duties

- To respond to the inspection specifications and draw up a tender.
- To set the inspection dates in consultation with the school.
- To brief the inspection team and to allocate responsibilities and duties.
- To meet parents before the inspection and to invite the appropriate authority (usually the governing body) to seek, if they wish, the views of all parents, using the standard parents' response form.
- To manage the collection of pre-inspection documentation and data.
- To plan the inspection timetable and to manage domestic arrangements for the inspection.
- To co-ordinate the inspection on site and liaise with the headteacher.
- To collate reports from individual inspectors and to maintain the record of evidence.
- To discuss the evidence and agree findings and recommendations with the inspection team.
- To prepare a report in accordance with the schedule and terms of the contract.
- To discuss the main findings separately with the senior management team and the governing body.
- To prepare a final report and summary report for submission to OFSTED and the governing body within 35 working days of the start of the inspection.

Inspection teams

Each inspection team will consist of a Registered Inspector, a lay inspector and team members. All inspectors must have been trained and accredited by OFSTED for the appropriate phase and type of school, whether secondary, primary (to include nursery) or special.

The team must be capable of inspecting the range of aspects of the school covered in the schedule, all the subjects of the National Curriculum and, in those schools which teach the subject to an agreed syllabus, religious education at appropriate levels. For the inspection of primary schools, a balance must be struck between phase and subject expertise, and similarly, teams inspecting special schools need a balance of specialisms to cover types of special need and subjects. Secondary school inspections must contain a balance of subject specialists and those competent to inspect broader school issues. Where a primary school or a secondary school has pupils with special needs, the inspection team should include one or more inspectors able to inspect the provision for those pupils. All teams will need to be of sufficient size to complete the collection of first-hand evidence in the school within the minimum number of inspector days prescribed in the Framework for Inspection.

Checklist of the team members' duties

- To take responsibility for curriculum and whole-school issues as required by the Registered Inspector.
- To collate and analyse pre-inspection documentation.
- To collect evidence at first hand.
- To record all observations clearly for the record of inspection.
- To discuss evidence and findings with other team members.
- To draft paragraphs of the final report as required.
- To assist the Registered Inspector at report-back meetings to the senior management team and governors, if required.

Lay inspectors

At least one member of the inspection team must be a person who has not been involved in the management of any school or the provision of education in any school, other than as a governor or in any other voluntary capacity (the lay inspector). However, present or former governors of the school to be inspected would not be eligible, because in the Act there are clauses referring to 'connection with the school' and the need to report impartially.

The assignments of lay inspectors will be negotiated with the Registered Inspector and should reflect their particular interests and expertise, and enable them to participate fully in the inspection. No aspect of the inspection is to be barred to a lay inspector. There are no rules as to how many days a lay inspector must be present during an inspection, but lay inspectors do have to complete successfully a course of training authorized by HMCI.

The purpose of the lay inspector is to provide a suitable, objective view of a school through the eyes of someone outside education – 'the commonsense view'. Interestingly, there would appear to be no point at which the lay inspector ceases to be regarded as a 'lay person', no matter how many inspections they have taken part in.

Governing bodies

Governors have a number of responsibilities in relation to the inspection process and, in a sense, they too are being inspected. The inspection report will include an evaluation of 'the effectiveness with which the governing body fulfils its legal responsibilities ... and the leadership of the governing body ...'.

Governors will need to work closely with the headteacher and staff of the school during the inspection process and their duties are as follows:

Before the inspection

- Comment on the specification form from OFSTED as a basis for tenders. While this must cover the full range of school activities, the governing body will be able to tell OFSTED about particular subjects offered outside the National Curriculum, the foreign languages taught, and any other facts which might require adjustment to the detail of the specification.
- Inform the parents of all registered pupils at the school.
- Inform the LEA (if an LEA school) or the Secretary of State (if a GM school).
- Inform those who appoint the school's foundation governors (if a voluntary school).
- Inform the local Training and Enterprise Council (TEC) and representatives of the local business community, in particular those who have employed former pupils (this applies to secondary only), and invite them to send any views on the school to the Registered Inspector.
- Arrange a meeting between the Registered Inspector and parents of pupils at the school, giving them at least three weeks' written notice. Note that governors, apart from parent governors, have no legal right to attend.

NB: The inspection of denominational religious education remains the responsibility of governors.

During the inspection

Inspectors will examine the school prospectus and development plan, and governors' policies on behaviour and discipline, spiritual and moral development, equal opportunities, special educational needs, and sex education. Further evidence examined will be governors' agendas and minutes of meetings, the governors' annual parents' report and the overall management of the budget and resources.

After the inspection

The Registered Inspector must discuss the main findings with the governing body, although these are not negotiable. The inspection findings should be presented in a manner which enables governors to identify clearly the features of the school which should be addressed in the action plan. Nothing which eventually appears in the published report should come as a surprise to the governing body.

When they receive the report and summary, the governing body must:

- make arrangements for all parents to have a copy of the summary report;
- make reasonable arrangements for the report and summary to be available for inspection by the public;
- provide a copy of the summary report free of charge on request to any member of the public;
- provide a copy of the full report to anyone who pays the prescribed fee;
- make sure the report's existence is widely known; sent to libraries, newspapers, radio stations, the TEC and local businesses;
- draw up an ACTION PLAN within 40 working days of receipt of the report with clear targets, time scales, success criteria and persons responsible;
- within 5 days of the completion of the action plan, send it to parents, all those employed at the school, OFSTED, the LEA, those who appoint foundation governors, if any, and make it available for inspection by any members of the public. They should also provide a single copy free of charge to any person living within a three-mile radius of the school who asks for one;
- include a statement of progress on the implementation of the action plan in every annual report to parents.

Checklist for governors

- Are the governing body aware of their roles and responsibilities during the inspection process?
- Are governors' policies up-to-date?
- What is the role of the governing body in the strategic management of the resources available to the school? How is this organized?
- Do they know in advance what major issues are likely to be raised?
- Are they already addressing concerns?
- What monitoring and evaluation procedures have the governors set in place?
- How far are governors involved in school development planning? Do they help set short-, medium- and long-term targets for the school?

Headteachers and staff

Schools will normally be informed by OFSTED of their inclusion in the inspection programme in the autumn term of the previous school year. OFSTED will write to governing bodies and headteachers well in advance of the term planned for the inspection, explaining the arrangements in more detail.

Before the inspection

Headteachers and governors must be consulted on the specification for the inspection of their school, and here heads and staff will want to work together to make sure that prospective tenderers are fully aware of the context of the school and extra details that are pertinent.

Once OFSTED has awarded the contract to a Registered Inspector, he or she must provide the head and governors with a list of information and documents that are needed in advance of the inspection. Pro forma need to be completed for the collection of standard information from each school. A list of additional documentation required is given in the *Handbook for the Inspection of Schools,* Part 3.

The Registered Inspector will make a preliminary visit or visits to the school to ensure that the head and staff know what information is needed and how best this can be made available. There will also be discussions on the process of the inspection itself and such precise details as the 'housing' of the team of inspectors during the inspection week. Clearly, schools will want to have reviewed their documentation well before this point; particularly whole-school policies and procedures and specific curriculum documentation.

During the inspection

The head, staff and governors must offer the Registered Inspector every opportunity to make a full and fair assessment of the school through the provision of necessary documents, ready access to school lessons, and activities and discussions with individuals and groups of pupils, staff and governors.

Lesson observation will constitute the major source of evidence, and teachers should be aware of the pro forma for lesson observation, the criteria and the grading system. They will want to demonstrate that their lesson planning is appropriate and matches that of the subject documentation generally and whole-school policies.

There will be opportunities for individuals and groups of staff to discuss policies, procedures and practices with inspectors, and this is another form of evidence. Consistency of practice will be the keynote here.

The head should liaise closely with the Registered Inspector throughout the inspection week. There will be subject feedback to heads of department and curriculum postholders.

After the inspection

There is no formal system of feedback to staff as a whole, apart from the senior management team. Staff governors will receive an oral report at the governors' meeting. (A summary of the inspection process appears on page 38.)

Checklist for heads and staff

- Prepare a thorough and succinct specification.
- Review whole-school documentation, planning and procedures.
- Establish levels of legal compliance.
- Examine the management of resources (time, money and staff).

- Study the inspection schedule with reference to evaluation criteria and evidence.
- Be clear about the pro forma for lesson observation, and for observation of work other than in lessons.
- Be fully aware of all the policies of the school.
- Review monitoring and evaluation systems.

Pupils

Little is said about the pupils' role during inspection, which is a little odd considering that they are central to the whole process. Certainly, heads and staff should consider how best to explain to their pupils the process they are about to become a part of. Pupils are involved in school inspections in three main ways (see below).

Observation

The inspection must allow for the observation of a wide range of lessons with pupils of all ages and abilities in all subjects and courses of the curriculum, which will often involve discussions with pupils. This will also involve observation in other school settings, such as assemblies, extracurricular activities and common areas of the school.

Oral evidence

No inspection of a school could take place without informal discussions with pupils, and on occasion these discussions will be formalized. Inspectors could ask to talk to a range of pupils about their work, the help and guidance available to them, and the part they play in the life of the school. These and other informal conversations in lessons, in the dining room, in the playground and around the school generally can help inspectors form a view about the quality of the school as a community.

Evidence of pupils' written and other work

Pupils' earlier, recent and current work provides a valuable source of evidence on standards and the progression of learning. As well as work seen during the observation of lessons, inspectors will examine in detail the work of a small sample of pupils who represent the age and ability range within the school.

Parents

Parents are involved in the inspection process in terms of being invited to attend a meeting before the inspection with the Registered Inspector, being invited to submit written comments by using a standard question-naire, and being entitled to receive a summary copy of the report after the inspection. Further, every annual report to parents subsequent to inspection must include a statement of the progress made in implementing the latest Action Plan.

The parents' meeting

Following the setting of dates for inspection, the governing body must arrange a meeting between the Registered Inspector and the parents. All parents of registered pupils at the school must be invited. Parents, for this purpose, include a local authority which looks after a child who is a registered pupil, within the meaning of the Children Act 1989.

The regulations require the governors to choose a date and time for the meeting likely to be convenient for as many parents as possible, and to serve them at least three weeks' notice in writing of the meeting.

The purpose of the meeting is for the Registered Inspector to explain and answer questions on the nature of the inspection and the report, and to seek parents' views about the school and the context in which it operates. It will be made clear at the start of the meeting that parents' views will be taken into account and may well influence the course of the inspection, but there can be no undertaking that they will be necessarily reflected in the report. Attendance at the meeting is limited to the Registered Inspector and other team members, and parents of registered pupils. The Secretary of State believes it is important that parents should have an opportunity to express their views to the inspector without the presence of those with direct responsibility for the school. The Registered Inspector should ensure that parents' views are sought on those aspects of the school which constitute particularly important evidence:

- pupils' progress and statements of work;
- the part parents play in the life of the school;
- the information which the school provides for parents, including reports;
- the help and guidance available to pupils;
- the values which the school promotes;
- homework;
- pupils' behaviour and attendance.

The parents' questionnaire

Parents may be invited to submit written comments to the Registered Inspector by using the standard parents' response form. This will cover the areas to be raised in the parents' meeting and allow for written comments on all other aspects of the school. The response form is available in twelve languages (*Handbook*, Part 3).

Evidence during the inspection

There may be opportunities for discussions with parents and the community during the inspection itself. Opportunities which arise for inspectors to observe a parents' evening, a careers convention or an exhibition, are valuable sources of direct evidence.

The inspector's report

The governing body must make arrangements for the parents of every registered pupil to be sent a copy of the summary report and make reasonable arrangements for the full report to be available for inspection. Schools may charge parents for copies of the full report.

Action plan

- The governing body must send the action plan within five days of its completion to the parents of all registered pupils.
- Every annual report to parents must include a statement of progress in implementing this plan.

Table 2.1 *The inspection process*

Before inspection

- OFSTED sends specification forms to the school.
- School completes this as a basis for tenders.
- OFSTED awards the contract.
- School informs parents and other agencies of the inspection.
- Registered Inspector negotiates dates with the school and collects appropriate documentation, and sets up the mechanics of the inspection.
- The governing body arranges a meeting between the Registered Inspector and parents. A questionnaire may be distributed to all parents.

During Inspection

Full and fair assessment of the school through the completion of a record of evidence which includes:
- Documentation and quantitative data.
- Lesson observation.
- Oral evidence.
- Pupils' written and other work.
- Subject/aspect summary sheets.
- Other evidence, including observations of general pupil activities and school meetings.

After inspection

- Debrief to the senior management team.
- Debrief to the governing body.
- Report and summary for parents sent to OFSTED within 35 working days of the start of the inspection.
- Governing body makes arrangements for all parents to get the summary report, and for the full report and summary to be available to the public generally and media outlets, according to the regulations.
- Governing body draws up an action plan within 40 working days with clear targets, time scales, success criteria and persons responsible.
- Governing body sends action plan to OFSTED and to parents within 5 days of its completion. They must also include a statement of progress in every annual report to parents.

Chapter 3

Reviewing Your Own School

Many heads and teachers in schools will explain that they constantly review their school by chatting to each other in the staff room. This style is somewhat reminiscent of Mr Pearson in *The Smith of Smiths*: 'I never read a book before reviewing it; it prejudices a man so'. Self-improving schools, however, have always used internal review. Now they can use the regular inspection cycle to validate their own processes.

Although much academic research and theoretical writing exists on school review, there is still a need for a set of practical suggestions on how to go about it. This chapter sets out to be practical yet rigorous in this vital area of the work of the school – vital if schools are to be self-improving societies in control of their own clear agendas, and not battered institutions, defeated by impossible external agendas. This is the main reason for reviewing your own school.

Schools review in order to answer the prime question: 'Are we doing the best we can for our children?' From this must follow the question: 'How do we know?' The answers to these questions can be found by detailed examination of the various aspects of school life. How do we set about this?

The processes

Most schools are very familiar with the processes of review. It is perhaps worth reminding ourselves that in order to carry out a review of any area, any subject, any department, any whole-school issue, there are four very clear parts to the process:

1 What are we doing now? *Gathering the evidence.*
2 What do we want to be doing? *Coming to a view of what might be.*
3 How do we get from where we are to where we want to be? *Action planning.*
4 How do we know when we have arrived at where we want to be? *Monitoring and evaluation.*

Monitoring is the process of making sure we are going in the right direction while we are travelling there. Evaluation is the process of establishing that we have arrived at where we want to be.

For many schools, this process has become a second nature to them during the school development planning cycle. Going through those processes is as natural as changing gear for an experienced driver. At the learning stage, changing gear and the four processes had to be consciously thought about.

The cycle

For a growing number of schools, the review process in its four parts is built into the school development planning cycle. For example, some schools now have their own four- or five-yearly cycle of school review. In a primary school, those responsible may decide in one year to review language in the autumn term, behaviour and discipline in the spring term and spiritual and moral development and RE in the summer term.

For the autumn term, they will have a plan which will first collect the evidence of where they are now and then, through discussion and dialogue, the school will come to a view of what it wants to be doing.

Towards the end of the autumn term, the school will turn its hopes and aspirations into an action plan within a time frame. The action plan will include monitoring and evaluation. This action plan with its dates can then be included into the next school development plan. It is important that the school identifies its own agenda in this way. Planning systematic and continuous review on the basis of an agreed long-term programme is different from the debilitating sense of constant changes of direction which schools need to guard against.

The link to external inspection

The external inspector has two important functions in the review process. First, an outside view of the school based on the gathering of evidence can be most helpful to those who are running the school. The criteria by which inspectors make their judgements based on the evidence are public and known to all. The second function which inspectors can helpfully perform is to bring a wider perspective to their judgement than the reviewer of one school can. They will be able to draw on observations made and comparisons gathered in a wide range of schools elsewhere.

The evaluation criteria in the Framework for a continuous process of review are a perfectly acceptable baseline for review; they link review and inspection helpfully together; they make the schools managers of their own inspection instead of victims of it; they empower schools to set their own priorities and not to be defeated by unreasonable external priorities.

The whole tone of a formal inspection of a school, where the systematic procedures of a school review are part of the culture of self-improvement, will be a very different tone from an inspection where school review either does not happen, or only happens sporadically, or is not happening in a serious way but people believe it to be happening because they talk to each other in staff rooms or offices.

Schools can manage an inspection in many ways and not be victims of it. The most important way is to set up what school governors from the business world often describe as internal audits, or as teachers would call it, a systematic and continuous process of school review. The inspection can then be a very helpful and insightful part of this review process.

The methodology

Rigour is an essential quality of serious school review. One of the ways of ensuring rigour is to look at the methodology of review for each of the four parts of the process.

1 What are we doing now? Gathering the evidence

Lesson observation*
Lesson observation is an important method of gathering evidence, see Chapter 5, pages 71–73 and OFSTED's schedule on pages 83–84. (Items

marked with an asterisk apply also to the fourth part of the review process, see pages 48–9.

Observation of other activities*

For example, if behaviour and discipline were being reviewed, a reviewer could gather evidence by observing the playground, the bus queue, breaks, corridors, a trip out of school, the arrival in school and departure from it. If spiritual, moral, social and cultural development was under review, the school reviewer might observe an assembly. If attendance was under review, the school reviewer might observe a registration period. If management and administration was under review, the school reviewer might attend a meeting to observe it against criteria. Just as with the lesson observation described in detail in Chapter 5, so the reviewers undertaking any other observation need to be clear what they are observing and for what purpose. Inspectors will use the OFSTED schedule in order to make whole-school judgements on the quality of teaching, the quality of learning and standards of achievement. They will also observe all other aspects from behaviour to accommodation.

'Pupil Pursuit'*

Following a pupil has become an increasingly popular method of gathering evidence in school reviews. In Chapter 8 a list of questions is given to answer during a 'pupil pursuit' in order to gather evidence on management, administration and efficiency. A 'pupil pursuit' could be used to gather evidence on the:

pupils' personal development and behaviour

behaviour and discipline in the school

pupils' spiritual, moral, social and cultural development

quality of teaching and learning

quality and range of the curriculum

assessment, recording and reporting

SEN (Special Educational Needs)

EO (Equal Opportunities)

standards of achievement

pupils' welfare and guidance

resources/accommodation

links with parents, agencies and other institutions

As with lesson observation, school reviewers need to be clear about what information they are trying to gather during the pursuit; what questions they should ask themselves in order to get that information; how to choose the pupil and what effect that will have on the evidence; how to prepare the pupil and teacher; whether or not to prepare teachers for the pursuit.

Reading documentation*
In any aspect of the school under review, the documentation needs to be read against the criteria of the Framework, and the particular aims and objectives of the school. It might be to see whether the particular documentation complies with statutory requirements, or if the documentation meets the evaluation criteria in the Framework, or if the documentation of a subject or a department matches whole-school policies, for example on SEN or EO or homework. See Figure 3.1.

Figure 3.1 *Match of policy to practice*

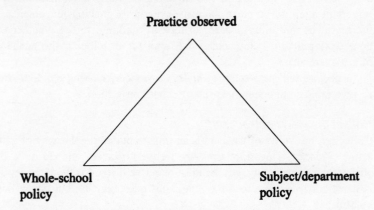

Practice observed

Whole-school policy

Subject/department policy

Match of Documentation to Practice Observed*
The match of departmental or subject documentation to whole-school policies will be an important area for inspectors. An inspector will also want to match the practice observed both to whole-school documentation and practice observed to subject or department documentation. Examples of subject and departmental handbooks and schemes of work are shown in Chapter 6, page 86.

Analysis of documentation*
In some areas it will not be sufficient to read the documentation; some

will need careful analysis. For example, both reviewer and inspector of the quality and range of the curriculum will want to analyse the timetable, the groupings, the time allocation, room usage and so on.

A reviewer or inspector of attendance will need to analyse data on attendance figures as well as read current registers.

Matrix
Using a matrix to analyse documentation can be helpful. See page 99.

Sampling of work*
Inspectors will, and reviewers can, sample children's work. The methods which HMI have traditionally used and inspectors may use are shown in Chapter 5, page 74. It is also possible to link a pupil pursuit to the sampling of work. Departments in a secondary school or year groups in a primary school may well decide to sample pupils' work. In all methods, it is important again to be clear about the criteria for making judgements. Is the reviewer sampling in order to look at marking; to see whether the homework policy is being consistently applied; or to look at the standards of achievement?

Inspectors will also sample children's work by hearing children read, an invariable component in a primary school inspection.

Collect the views of teachers*
Collecting the views of teachers is an important and regular way of gathering evidence. Questionnaires are frequently used, and do have the advantage of anonymity, but the most effective method is the interview. It is more costly in time than the ubiquitous questionnaire, but much more helpful.

Interviewing a teacher to collect evidence can take many forms of questioning and listening. The interviewer who is trying to find evidence about a specific area might have very precise questions. A school reviewer who is asking questions about a more pervasive part of the Framework, such as management and planning, might use the technique of questioning described in Chapter 8, pages 127–9. The reviewer uses questions about the process of meetings in the school, for example, in order to gather evidence about consultation, decision-making, strategic planning, line management and all the other aspects of management and planning. Interviewing teachers in both the ways described will form an important part of the inspection process.

Collect the views of pupils*

Inspectors will collect the views of pupils: they will talk to children in the lessons they observe; they will talk to children as they move about the school and observe its daily business; they might ask to interview a sample of pupils; they might ask to interview the pupils whose work they have been given as the school sample of written work.

The school reviewer can do all these things, but there are inherent problems for the reviewer. The pupils primarily know the reviewer as a member of staff. Some colleague teachers might feel threatened unless the whole business was handled carefully. For everyone, the Framework has a warning about intrusion into spiritual and moral issues which some families might find offensive. It also notes that it is important not to confuse culture, ethnicity and particular religious belief.

One of the obvious and safe areas for a school reviewer to collect evidence from pupils is their attitude to learning. It is quite appropriate and straightforward to ask questions such as:

(a) Which subjects do you find easiest?
(b) Why is that?
(c) What sort of work do you find easiest?
(d) Why is that?
(e) What do you do if you get stuck?
(f) Do you like working in groups?
(g) Do you like working on your own?
(h) Do you like helping other people who are finding work hard?
(i) How hard do you find homework?
(j) What encourages you most when you are working?

Collect the views of governors and parents

Inspectors will be collecting the views of the governing body and of parents. School reviewers have similar problems in interviewing these groups to those they have when interviewing pupils.

The omnipresent questionnaire to gather information from parents needs very careful management if it is to provide accurate and helpful information. Interviews with a sample of governors and of parents are costly in time, but need to be as representative as possible.

The OFSTED questions for parents are very specific. The school reviewer can use specific questions in a certain area, for example, questions on assessment and reporting to parents. Alternatively, they can be of the core question variety described above to investigate a wider area, such as relationships with parents and communication with parents.

Conduct a spot check*

School reviewers often find this a good way to collect evidence. A spot check on attendance can illuminate the effectiveness of the monitoring of attendance. A reviewer in a department might decide to spot check, with the consent of the department, all the written work in one year group.

Inspectors can and will undertake spot checks.

Sampling of pupils*

In order to follow through one area in the school, it is possible to take some case studies of pupils who, for example, have special needs, have had poor attendance or have had behavioural difficulties. The reviewer can read the file and review the case study to illuminate the school's management of one of these areas.

Transect study*

In Chapter 5, page 75, a transect is described as a method of internal review. It is particularly helpful in curriculum areas and for departments and subjects.

Look at resources/accommodation*

A school reviewer can easily look at resources and accommodation, or ask others to take part in a structured survey. The Framework gives some criteria, but schools may have some in addition.

2 What do we want to be doing? – coming to a view of what might be

Some practical suggestions for reviewing this question are:

- debate among the teachers in the normal meeting forum;
- talking to individual teachers;
- discussions with other groups, governors and parents;
- discussion papers with various options put forward;
- visit another school or teacher or department which has good practice in the area being reviewed;
- INSET
  In service training can be held for whole staff or subgroups. Alternatively, one teacher might attend some specific INSET to gather infor-

mation for the school and then come back to disseminate the INSET to other members of staff.

- Learning from a critical friend
The school's critical friend has traditionally been the LEA adviser, but in the future this generic title might encompass other persons. Whatever may happen to the LEA advisory services, every school should seek out a critical friend. This critical friend should bring knowledge of the practice of others, of new ideas and of what can be achieved for the school or for the department.

Underpinning all these very practical and obvious ways of achieving a view of 'where we want to be', must be a positive attitude associated with self-improving schools.

There are four main points here: most teachers in self-improving schools believe that they can change things for the better through their own attitudes and then their own actions. They have the confidence to accept that some aspects could be better. They have the broad understanding that their practice is part of a wider curriculum. They have a belief that schools improve themselves by teamwork.

Whereas inspectors and school reviewers both collect evidence in the first part of the process described above, in this second part, inspectors and reviewers differ. Inspectors, in making a judgement on the first part, 'Where is the school now?', obviously make a judgement based on the evidence against the Framework criteria and their wide knowledge of many schools. In that sense they are mentally comparing a school in its present position with others. In the second part of the process, 'What do we want to be doing – coming to a view of what might be', the inspectors play no part and are very different from the school reviewers. The school reviewer is undertaking the second part of the whole process of review.

3 How do we get from where we are to where we want to be?

Action planning
Many schools do this successfully. It is not a difficult process to make an action plan, but it needs to be done systematically. It is a matter of turning very specific ideas, which we have arrived at through meetings, debate and the normal round of dialogue and consultation, into a plan. See Figure 3.2, which shows what a simple and effective format might look like.

Figure 3.2   *A simple action plan*

MAIN TARGET: To get attendance rates up by 2% in Years 9, 10 and 11				
Subtarget	Who is to be Responsible	Action by When	Review Dates by When	
Publish weekly data				
Heads of year to receive allocated clerical hours				
Investigate optical mark reader for registration				
Etc				

The inspector's job does not include this area of action planning.

4 How do we know when we have arrived at where we want to be?

This fourth part is as essential to the whole process of review as any other part.

Monitoring and evaluation

In the past, monitoring and evaluation have tended to be a weak area in many departments and schools; but once it is built into the culture of a self-improving school, it becomes second nature and an integral part of the whole cycle of school review. Development planning implies knowing whether a goal has been reached: evaluation is answering the question, 'How do we know that we have arrived at where we want to be? Monitoring is answering the question as we proceed, 'Are we moving in the right direction to where we want to be?'

To answer these questions, we need to gather evidence. Many of the methods used in gathering the evidence for the first part of the process of review can be used to gather the evidence in this fourth part of the process (see pages 41–46). In using these methods, the reviewer is collecting information to establish whether a target has been reached.

Targets

If a target was, for example, to improve attendance in Years 9 to 11 by 2 per cent in a year, then it is a simple matter of analysing the attendance data and seeing if the target increase has been achieved. If the departmental target was to ensure that every teaching area had attractive, stimulating displays which also celebrated children's work, then it is simple to observe display work in each room against the three criteria.

Where targets are wider-ranging, it is important to turn a qualitative pious hope into specific hard detail. If the school sets itself the target of raising its profile in the community, it will find that such an aspiration is impossible to evaluate seriously. By turning that aspiration into specific targets, such as (a) organising a carol concert for three contributory schools; (b) producing an attractive and interesting school newsletter once a half-term; and (c) clearing the school grounds of litter, then the school can both monitor and evaluate its success against any specific detailed targets. It is helpful to staff and a useful signal to inspectors for statements about the school's monitoring and evaluation policy and strategies to be included in the school development plan, the staff handbook and departmental handbooks.

It is also important to involve the governors in some way in the process of monitoring and evaluation. A governor could be asked to give oral evidence to the reviewer and the governing body could also receive succinct evaluation reports on progress towards meeting a target, probably built into the development planning year cycle.

The particular challenges of reviewing your own school

These challenges are mainly centred on the first part of the process, gathering the evidence to answer the question, 'What are we doing now?' The challenges seem to fall into 6 principal categories:

1 Time

Gathering evidence costs time. The task needs to be broken down into manageable activities – as, of course, does the review itself. No school can use, or needs to use, all the different methodologies described in this Chapter. Choose different methods of gathering evidence for different areas which the school is reviewing. The delegated INSET budget can be used to fund classroom observation. Some extra clerical hours can be bought in with a delegated budget in one month to deal with analysing data for evidence gathering. A routine meeting of a subject or a department can be designated for sampling children's work.

The importance of building the reviewing cycle into the school development plan (SDP) will make review an inherent part of school life. There is a cost, and some of the time cost can be met through the strategies listed below. One of the ways of overcoming some part of the time problem is to ask a critical friend, for example the LEA adviser, to carry out some of the gathering of information within the context of the school review.

2 *Difficulties in knowing about the wider context or of examples of good practice*

It is difficult for teachers who commit themselves to one school every day to know about others' practice and to have a sense of where their school's practice fits in a wider context. Teachers do visit other schools and this can be helpful, but because their first commitment is to their own pupils, it is a limited strategy. The critical friend, an adviser, can be particularly helpful in sharing good practice and in contextualizing the school's own practice.

3 *Old eyes – new eyes*

The challenge of seeing any aspect of the school's life through fresh eyes is very hard for people who have been there some time. It is analogous to walking into a house on the day you purchase it. The new owner sees things the ex-owner has stopped seeing. One of the distinguishing features of self-improving schools is the capacity to see familiar things with fresh eyes, not to collude with the status quo. The Framework provides clear criteria to give the school reviewer a rigour to see all aspects with new eyes. Wise schools will take advantage of the new eyes coming in to them: newly qualified teachers, supply teachers and new appointments.

4 *The old familiar faces*

One of the most difficult challenges for the school reviewer is that he or she is involved in making judgements which involve colleague teachers. The two tools which can assist here are, first, again using clearly agreed, clearly stated, rigorous criteria for the collection of evidence; second, a reviewing school needs to concentrate on reviewing areas such as attendance or mathematics or cross-curricular themes. It is not appraising individuals. Trust, confidence and clear ground rules will assist in the process of reviewing aspects of school life and in not making judgements on individuals.

5 Role of the governing body

In an inspection, the governing body (GB) has an important role to play. In school review, each school needs to decide what role it wishes its governing body to play. These roles will vary from simply underwriting the completed review programme in the long term and in the SDP, to receiving a report on the action plan of the review of an area, to some member of the GB being asked to simulate the role of the lay inspector in a school review for the gathering of evidence part of the process. In linking review to inspection, it is vital that the GB does receive regular reports of reviews. In their counsel of perfection, nothing which OFSTED inspectors say to the GB should come as a surprise to them if they are locked in, by receiving regular reports, to the school's systematic cycle of review.

6 The challenge of the expertise

A great mystique has surrounded inspection. Inspecting and reviewing are hard, but so is teaching. The outside reviewer or inspector has the benefit of time allocated and of time to practise the skills. The school reviewer has to find the time, and GEST (Grant for Education, Support and Training) delegated budgets are invaluable; if this is not training then nothing is. School reviewers will not have the practice of doing the work frequently but they can establish clear criteria against which to gather evidence. The Framework is a marvellous document for school improvement. The school reviewers can be the lead people in turning an OFSTED inspection into both a catalyst for school improvement, and a part of the school's systematic cycle of review. The self-reviewing school will become the manager and collaborator of an inspection, and not the victim of it.

Chapter 4
Standards and Quality Achieved
(Framework Reference 3.1)

According to the OFSTED evaluation criteria, standards of achievement are to be judged by 'evaluating the evidence of what pupils know, understand and can do in the subjects of the curriculum, including the knowledge, skills and understanding defined in the attainment targets and programmes of study of National Curriculum subjects and agreed syllabuses for Religious Education; and by pupils' competence across the curriculum in the key skills of reading, writing, speaking and listening, and numeracy'.

Inspectors will assess the quality and standards being achieved, and the results of national assessments and examinations in relation to national norms. They will assess separately whether these standards are appropriate to the pupils' ages and abilities. There may of course be special circumstances in particular schools which may affect standards of achievement, but comments about these and judgements about their significance in the social context of the school should be clearly separated from the presentation of the results.

In the OFSTED amplification of the evaluation criteria, a school with high standards is where 'the great majority of pupils show high achievement in most areas of work' and 'where standards are satisfactory or better pupils achieve standards which are at least commensurate with what is known of their potential ... with little variation in different subject areas and activities'. In a school with low standards of achievement, 'most pupils are working at levels significantly below those normally attained by pupils of similar age elsewhere' and 'where overall standards are unsatisfactory standards are likely to vary considerably between subjects and the performance of individual pupils is likely to be significantly different in various aspects of their work'. In special schools and schools having pupils with statements of special education need, good standards are found when the great majority of pupils show high achievement in most areas of work, taking into account any disabilities, and unsatisfactory standards are found when there is evidence of underachievement, variable standards across subjects and poor individual performance, taking into account any effect of disability.

When assessing standards of achievement, every aspect of the school listed in the schedule for inspection is to be evaluated in terms of its impact upon pupils' standards of achievement and quality of work, and there are a number of key statements and judgements under different schedule headings that schools should take note of with regard to their own review processes:

- 'An indication of the extent to which the standards achieved are commensurate with the age and capabilities of pupils'.
- 'An evaluation of pupils' learning, including gains in knowledge, understanding and skills; an evaluation of their competence as learners: and an evaluation of their attitudes to learning'.
- 'A summative assessment of the value for money provided by the school in terms of the quality, standards, efficiency and effectiveness of the school in relation to the level of financial resources available to it'.
- 'The extent to which behaviour has an effect on standards of achievement, the quality of learning and the quality of life in the school'.
- 'An evaluation of the quality of teaching provided and its effects on the quality of learning and standards of pupils' achievements'.
- 'An evaluation of the accuracy and consistency of assessment and a judgement of the extent to which assessment of the work of individual pupils is used to promote higher standards'.
- 'A judgement on the effectiveness of curriculum provision achievement in terms of its impact on the quality of learning and standards'.
- 'An evaluation of the school's policy and practice for equality of opportunity and its effects on the quality of learning and standards of achievement'.
- 'An evaluation of the quality of learning and standards achieved by pupils with special educational needs'.

- 'An evaluation of the availability and deployment of staff ... and consequent effects on the quality and standards of pupils' work'.
- 'A judgement on the effects of the availability, accessibility, quality and use of resources on standards of achievement and the quality of learning'.
- 'An evaluation of how the availability, accessibility, management, use and condition of the accommodation affect standards of pupils' work on the quality of learning'.
- 'An evaluation of the effect of community links and liaison arrangements on the quality of learning and standards of achievement'.

In a very real sense, therefore, everything that the school does should be related to the sustained improvement of the quality and standards of pupils' work, and schools should seek to demonstrate this connection through documentation and practice. School review and inspection is fundamentally concerned with raising standards across the whole ability range, and to do that it is essential that schools are able to measure achievement both in what pupils know, understand and can do, and also to record that achievement in the fullest sense.

Analysis of achievement data

In terms of the inspection process, standards of achievement gauged by the National Curriculum assessments and examination results will be established before an inspection by comparing the achievement of results with the latest set of reference norms provided by HMCI.

School data and indicators will include a summary of the National Curriculum assessments and the results of public examinations for each of the two years prior to the inspection, set in the context of local and national statistics. From their analysis will emerge a general picture of the overall standard compared with national achievements and those of pupils in *similar* schools, and an early indicator of standards in particular subjects.

Clearly, schools will wish to demonstrate that they analyse standards of achievement in a similar way as part of their practice, and various standards have to be borne in mind such as:

- trends over time
- comparisons with
  LEA results
- comparisons with
  similar schools
- comparisons with
  national statistics

- difference of performance   - achievement of ethnic
   in each subject area   minority groups
- relative achievement
   of boys and girls

As part of monitoring and evaluation, all schools should set out their methods and techniques for analysing National Curriculum assessments and public examinations. The exploration of patterns and anomalies should be sought through weighing up a range of interactive factors, and this diagnosis of results should lead to a review of attitudes and practice.

Checklist of questions for review (whole school)

1 Is there an appropriate emphasis on academic achievement in the school?
2 Is the assessment of the work of individual pupils used to promote higher standards?
3 What assumptions are made about pupils' abilities, and how widely shared are these?
4 Can these assumptions be substantiated?
5 Are the diverse needs of all pupils being met?
6 What scope is there for improvement? What are the major constraints? What are the chances of overcoming them?
7 What practical steps can be taken to raise attainment for all? What changes are needed in terms of:
   - methods of teaching and learning?
   - teacher expectations?
   - organization of teaching groups?
   - special provision?
   - use of the library and resources?
   - study skills?
   - setting and monitoring homework?
   - procedures for monitoring and assessing progress?
   - the suitability of courses?
8 Is there an action plan to raise achievement with short-, medium- and long-term targets?
9 What needs to be done to explain the changes and promote support for them among:
   - the whole staff?
   - governors?

– all pupils?
– all parents?

Similarly, subject areas will need to set out how they analyse standards of achievement, first establishing a clear set of data based upon results over a period of time compared to LEA and national results, and including other evidence such as the policy on examination entry and analysis of results of ethnicity and gender. These subject areas should also look at ways of improving attainment through organizational curriculum change and teaching and learning strategies such as:

- improving the classroom climate/learning environment;
- more precise diagnosis of learning needs;
- better monitoring and record keeping;
- extra reinforcement of learning;
- more opportunities for individuals to discuss their work with teachers;
- enrichment strategies;
- coursework and homework 'clinics';
- review of teaching styles;
- raising pupil expectations.

Some methods that can be used for internal school review are set out in Table 4.1, pp.65–68).

Value added

Judgements of whether standards are as high as could reasonably be expected rely on evaluating pupils' achievement relative to their age and abilities, and gauging the progress made or value added. Where possible, relative standards will be judged against evidence of the earlier attainment of pupils on entry to the school if known, or at the end of a previous key stage. To gauge value added effectively, inspectors will need to examine the evidence that the school produces on prior ability and value added as well as National Curriculum and assessment data. It is clearly important that all schools keep this issue under review and are able to document and articulate the progress of individuals and groups of pupils in the whole curriculum as well as in individual subjects. The principle that assessment should be subjected to an added value analysis is now accepted, although the techniques are often complex and their interpretation depends upon a number of assumptions and qualifications. To help inspectors in this task, OFSTED issues a Pre-Inspection Content and School Indicator (PICSI) report which sets the school in its local context and compares it with other schools.

The statistical treatment of added value is comparative in approach. It attempts to estimate the influence of a school by comparing the achievements of pupils in relation to a number of factors, the most important of which is prior ability. The best approaches to this look at the relationship between prior ability and achievement for each *individual* pupil, although this all depends on the availability of information on pupils' prior attainments, which varies according to the educational phase. At the moment, evidence of prior learning can be taken variously from:

- pre-school attainments
- nursery records
- reading tests at various ages
- verbal reasoning scores at 11
- internal testing at entry to the school

- Standard Attainment Tests at the end of key stages
- records of achievement
- accreditation of prior learning, particularly in vocational qualifications

It is in every school's interests to develop value added measures which can be used with confidence as an internal quality assurance procedure. There are of course a number of projects which help schools to do this, particularly in secondary education, for example ALIS (the A Level Information System) and YELLIS (the Year 11 Information System). The ALIS system provides a data base with fair performance indicators for such aspects of A Level provision as effectiveness in examinations, measuring A Levels against GCSE scores, but also indicating rates of participation in extra-curricular activities, students' attitudes and processes such as class sizes, teaching strategies and homework. Similarly, the YELLIS system provides a data base matching GCSE grades to tests taken before entry to the secondary school, but also taking into account other process factors.

Some primary schools have begun to examine value added using attitudinal and behavioural measures and taking into account gender, ethnicity and the first language of the pupils, although these are measures dependent on their context, and cognitive achievement within the National Curriculum is a vital component of progress. Possible measures to be identified are:

- SATs results at KS1
    and KS2
- internal school assessments

- self-esteem
- attitude to school
- deprivation index

Expressed in its most general form, the added value of a school is the contribution that school makes to the development of each of its pupils, which is often used in relation to their academic achievements. Obviously, there are other indices of achievement and these would include pupil attitudes such as:

- enjoyment
- tolerance
- co-operation
- ability to tackle
    problems

- development of
    wider interests
- attendance and
    punctuality
- career aspirations

and pupil experiences and successes in the ethical, aesthetic and physical areas of the curriculum and outside the formal curriculum. Evidence for these in school can be obtained through first-hand observation, talking with pupils and an examination of records of achievement, and schools should attempt to explain and write down their view of value added in those areas that are not so easily measured. Having given due regard to different forms of achievement, schools will also wish to explain and write down, both collectively and in subject areas, their analysis of value added in terms of how the *school* is making a difference to assessment outcomes rather than the *prior attainments* of pupils which it happens to have within its walls. In terms of standards of achievement, a school's position in an overall league table is not as important as its relative performance when compared to similar schools, both locally and across the country. Clearly, however effective a school might be, if most of its pupils are drawn from, and grouped within, lower bands of attainment, it would have considerable difficulty in matching the assessment outcomes of a school whose pupils were mostly drawn from the higher bands. Account needs to be taken of the different profiles of pupils within each school in order to assess the value added effect of the school.

Lesson observation

The OFSTED pro forma for lesson observation contains a section on standards of achievement by pupils in their work as observed in lessons, and inspectors will make a graded judgement of pupils' standards and achievements in relation to national norms. Where possible, they will also comment on pupils' achievements in relation to their ages and abilities and any special circumstances, and a numerical grade will be given for this judgement as well. Observation should focus on standards being achieved by pupils engaged in their work, and whether the standard of work achieved is appropriate to pupils' capabilities estimated from other evidence such as their previous output, and views formed in discussion with them. Instances of underachievement, where pupils show themselves to be capable of one standard and performing at a lower standard, and who are denied the opportunity of improving, will also be recorded. In particular, the following aspects of pupils' work make up the criteria by which standards of achievement will be judged:

– knowledge and understanding	– reading
	– writing
– acquisition of skills	– calculating
– speaking and listening	– problem-solving

and the specific knowledge, skills and understanding defined in the attainment targets and programmes of study of National Curriculum subjects as set down in course programmes.

For example, in mathematics, pupils need to show knowledge, skills and understanding in number, algebra, shape and space, and handling data. The evaluation of pupils' achievement must also take into account evidence of pupils' ability:

– to remember relevant mathematical knowledge;
– to perform the skills and operations necessary to achieve the required results;
– to understand what they are doing;
– to tackle a range of tasks involving practical work, investigational work and problem-solving, using the required mathematical concepts, skills and facts.

In science, a judgement on standards of achievement should be made in the context of the attainment targets and:

– evidence of pupils' knowledge and understanding of scientific ideas;
– the development of specific methods of investigation;

- the appreciation of the nature of scientific knowledge;
- understanding of the contribution science makes to society;
- ability to communicate scientific findings through mathematical and graphical skills and the use of computers.

In English, the evaluation of standards reached should be based on evidence of pupils' command of the three essential literacy skills of speaking and listening, reading and writing, and also the skills of spelling, handwriting and presentation, and pupils':

- awareness of the interrelationship of these skills;
- using their proficiency in one or more of these to improve the quality of their work in other skills;
- recognition that first attempts at language tasks can be improved by critical reworking;
- use of a variety of good literature;
- recognition of the power of language and the relationship between language and thought.

It is important that teachers familiarize themselves with the criteria for judging standards of achievement in all subject areas, and become able both to assess them for themselves and others as appropriate in the teaching and learning situation and in the examination of pupils' work. Every lesson that is planned should have the objective of raising standards of achievement, and this focus should also be referred to in schemes of work.

Standards of achievement in relation to skills in different subject areas and across the curriculum can be tabulated, and teachers should have clear ideas and strategies on how they are going to develop achievement levels in those skill areas. A common core of skills described in the inspection schedule would be the following:

- writing
- reading
- speaking and listening
- calculating and tabulating
- using number
- spelling

- graphicacy
- design and making
- information technology
- performing
- problem-solving
- presentation
- personal and social

and the six core skills referred to in the National Curriculum are condensed to:

- communication   - problem-solving
- numeracy   - personal and social
- study skills   - information technology

As well as knowledge and understanding defined in the attainment targets and programmes of study of the National Curriculum and other courses, pupils need to demonstrate competence in specific subjects and cross-curricular skills.

These standards of achievement in terms of pupil competences will be recorded by inspectors in the way shown below, on a seven-point scale, for example:

Speaking and listening
Excellent   x x x x x x x   Poor
KS1

A review exercise in school could begin to establish a perspective of where pupils are on these different continua and this would help the school in working towards improvements in particular areas.

Pupils' work

Part of the record of evidence relating to standards of achievement is the sampling of a range of pupils' work done over a period of time, as well as the examination of pupils' work in the learning areas while lessons are taking place. The former activity can easily be done by teachers as a monitoring of standards exercise by selecting work from the least able, average and most able pupils across a class or year group. This exercise will reveal standards and skills in different subject areas and will be particularly useful in examining pupils' competence across the curriculum in the key skill areas of literacy, oracy and numeracy. Whether done through inspection or internal review, this exercise will enable judgements to be made on both standards attained concurrently by the same pupils in the various subjects of the curriculum and the extent and rate of improvements in standards by pupils of different abilities in the various subjects.

Discussion with pupils about their work should further demonstrate their own awareness of their levels of achievement and their understanding of strengths and weaknesses in their work. It should also reveal their confidence or otherwise in the means to improve, their perceptions of what major factors determine their standards of achievement, and their own explanation of fluctuations from term to term or subject to subject.

Profiles/records of achievement

In order to obtain a full picture of standards of achievement, inspectors will wish to examine the full range of pupil achievement, and this can be seen in most secondary schools and some primary schools through pupils' profiles and records of achievement. Not only do these records provide a more rounded picture of pupil achievement by helping pupils to take greater responsibility for their own learning and set realistic plans for the future, they also help the school identify and provide specific elements of courses and activities that enhance the development of pupils' skills and abilities. Ideally, records of achievement should be seen to be contributing to pupils' personal development and progress by improving their motivation and self-esteem.

Schools need to consider carefully how they define and recognize achievement rather than reinforce failure, and a dynamic profiling system including staff, pupils and parents can be a powerful agent in establishing a climate of success across the full range of pupil activities – including academic, sporting and caring. One of the advantages of giving formal credit for a wide range of activities is that pupils may be encouraged to see as worthwhile some of the achievements which have hitherto appeared to be of little value. Even small advances can be recognized and accredited, serving a dual function of crediting success and recognizing achievement, and motivating pupils to improve their academic attainment. A school needs to demonstrate how it fosters a climate of high expectations and to show that it is producing pupils motivated to participate and achieve with improved self-confidence and enhanced self-worth.

Two strategies

Method 1   whole-school strategies for reviewing standards of achievement

1 Define and describe standards of achievement in the context of the school relative to national and local norms. This should be set out in a

strategy document.

2 Detailed, systematic review of all National Curriculum assessments and public examination results as part of an annual school audit and an ongoing monitoring and evaluation system of standards of achievement. Outcomes to be shared with staff and governors, including causes for celebration as well as causes for concern, and an action plan established on the basis of clear evidence.

3 Lines of accountability to be clearly established as between the governing body, senior management team, curriculum postholders/heads of department and all teachers, and success criteria to be agreed.

4 Checks on the teacher assessment system and what are established as assessed pieces of work. Moderation of standards through a link member of the senior management team as well as members of the subject area.

5 Monitor homework across the school and its role in improving standards.

6 Review grouping strategies across the school, based upon evidence of success/failure. Establish cohorts of students who will work together to achieve improving standards.

7 Review enrichment programmes and special provision designed to enhance learning opportunities. Are they adequate? When they are established do they make a difference?

8 Establish ways of spreading good practice by sharing successful experiences – develop appropriate INSET which focuses ways of improving pupil achievement.

9 Examine the study skills that are built into the programme of work. Is there evidence of successful outcomes? What else needs to be done in terms of whole-school curriculum planning?

10 Are all pupils competent in the use of information technology? Can all pupils find extra information for themselves?

11 Regularly sample work of pupils of different ages and abilities across the curriculum, including work displayed and homework, and feed back observation on standards.

12 Regularly sample records of pupils' progress and attainment, including any self-assessments made by pupils.

Method 2   improving achievement in the subject/learning area

1 Setting appropriate targets and learning objectives in lessons and schemes of work related to improving standards.

2 Regularly reviewing pupils' work and improving procedures for diagnosing learning needs and for monitoring progress.

3 Changing criteria for defining and assessing attainment. How does the subject area define and reward achievement?

4 More practical and activity-based approaches to teaching and learning, and evidence of what works best for particular subjects.

5 Raising expectations and workload, and challenging pupils to achieve.

6 Review and reorganization of teaching groups to create the best learning situation for pupils. In what circumstances are mixed-ability teaching, setting or banding most appropriate? What type of pupil groupings appear to yield the best achievements? Is this consistent for all subject areas?

7 Extension and enrichment of learning opportunities. How are pupils given extended learning opportunities and how are they given extra help? Are there support 'clinics' for pupils to refer to? Are there learning resource packs for them to enrich their experiences and stimulate higher achievement?

8 Setting targets for achievement in the subject. What percentage of pupils can improve their SATs scores? What percentage of pupils can obtain the higher grades of GCSE passes? Running regular quick checks as to whether pupils are on target to achieve or exceed practical grades.

9 Action plans for all departments/subject areas to lever up achievement describing the organizational, teaching and learning techniques that are to be followed as a corporate activity.

10 Improve the learning environment in the subject area so that pupils are motivated to achieve and to return to that environment at lunch and after school to extend themselves further.

Table 4.1 *Standards and quality achieved*

What School can do for Internal Review		What Inspectors can do	Fwk Ref
For Whole School	**For Department/ Curriculum/Area**		
Analyse National Curriculum assessments and examination results and compare these with national norms, similar schools and results over other years Set appropriate whole-school targets for improvement	Indicate standards in particular subjects in comparison to similar schools and national norms – set appropriate subject targets for improvement	Study pre-inspection data on the standards of pupils' achievements in National Curriculum assessment and examinations to obtain a general picture compared with national achievements and those of pupils in similar schools	3.1
Analyse the relative achievements of boys and girls and ethnic minority groups across the curriculum Devise strategies to tackle anomalies	Analyse the achievement of boys and girls and ethnic minority groups in the subject area and compare to national data where possible Devise strategies to tackle anomalies	Examine patterns and trends across the curriculum and in subject areas in terms of the achievement of boys and girls and ethnic minority groups	3.1
Define and describe the value added element of pupils' achievements across the curriculum Relate to prior attainment of pupils	Analyse the progress made by individual pupils in the subject area with reference to general ability	Inspect pupils' achievement in relation to their general abilities and gauge the progress made or value added benefit	3.1

Table 4.1 continued

What School can do for Internal Review		What Inspectors can do	Fwk Ref
For Whole School	**For Department/ Curriculum/Area**		
Illustrate how the diagnosis of results leads to curricular and organizational modifications in the school	Illustrate how the diagnosis of results in the subject area is used to improve teaching and learning	Inspect the effectiveness of the monitoring and evaluation of pupil achievement	3.1
Review all aspects of the schedule for inspection in terms of the contribution made to pupils' standards of achievement and quality of work	Review all aspects of the schedule in terms of the impact made on pupil performance in the subject area	Evaluate every aspect of the school listed in the schedule in terms of the impact on the pupils' standards of achievement and quality of work	3.1
Review pupils' competence across the curriculum in the key skills of literacy, oracy and numeracy	Evaluate the contribution of teaching and learning in the subject to literacy, oracy and numeracy	Make a clear comment and judgement on standards across the curriculum in literacy, oracy and numeracy	3.1
Review and analyse standards of achievement in lessons across the curriculum Observe lessons with set criteria in mind related to standards of achievement	Keep under review standards achieved by pupils engaged in their work with reference to particular subject skills	Inspect and grade the standard of achievement in every lesson observed with reference to what pupils know, understand and can do, and whether the standard of work pupils are achieving is appropriate to their capabilities	3.1

Table 4.1 continued

| What School can do for Internal Review | | What Inspectors can do | Fwk Ref |
For Whole School	For Department/ Curriculum/Area		
Review standards attained concurrently by the same pupils in the various subjects of the curriculum Sample work across all subjects on a systematic basis	Review and sample standards of pupils' work in subject areas across ages, key stage and abilities Moderate this across the subject area/ department	Scrutinize work completed over a period of time by a sample of pupils of different ages and abilities, and reach a judgement on standards attained	3.1
Require subject leaders to produce evidence of regular checks with pupils on their work	Discuss with pupils across the ability range on a regular basis their perceptions and understanding of achievement levels	Discuss aspects of the work examined with the pupils who produced it and explore pupils' awareness of their levels of achievement in the various subjects and their understanding of particular strengths and weaknesses in their work	3.1
Examine instances of underachievement across the curriculum and suggest whole-school strategies to combat this	Examine instances of underachievement across different teaching groups in the subject, analyse the reasons for this and suggest solutions	Record instances of underachievement where pupils are performing at a lower standard or are denied the opportunity of improving	3.1
Analyse where achievement levels are highest and how consistent this is across the curriculum	Examine instances of high achievement across different teaching groups	Record instances of high achievement and look out for a consistent pattern of high achievement across the curriculum	3.1

Table 4.1 continued

| What School can do for Internal Review | | What Inspectors can do | Fwk Ref |
For Whole School	For Department/ Curriculum/Area		
Define and describe the concept of achievement as applied by the whole school Link to records of achievement and methods of celebrating success	Define and describe the concept of achievement as applied in the subject area How is this recorded?	Give credit to the full range of achievement as well as academic achievement	3.1

Chapter 5

Quality of Teaching and of Learning

Framework References 7.1 and 3.2

Teaching and learning are at the very heart of a school. In a typical secondary class, 29,000 hours of learning occur in an academic year. In a typical primary class, 25,000 hours occur. Evaluating teaching and the quality of learning against criteria has not been a frequent activity. It will become more frequent as schools prepare themselves for inspection and learn to use inspection as a catalyst for self-improvement. A good school will keep the quality of teaching and the quality of learning under constant review.

In the classroom observation schedule, which inspectors will use and with which schools are already working in focused ways, the quality of teaching is evaluated separately from the quality of learning, which in turn is evaluated separately from the standards of achievement. There are now two grades for standards of achievement, one assessed against national norms on a 5-point scale. The other standards of achievement grade is assessed in relation to pupils' capabilities on a 5-point scale. Appended to this chapter is the OFSTED observation schedule and their definition of the grades. The grade definitions are common definitions for quality of teaching, quality of learning and standards of achievement. It is possible to have very good teaching in a lesson, say a grade 1 or 2, very good learning, again a grade 1 or 2, and standards of achievement of both or either types by children which are less than satisfactory, say a 4. How? There are various factors that could cause this, but an obvious combination would be a high performance of the teacher and a positive struggling attitude of the learners, but only basic competence in language which was limiting the standard of their achievement.

Conversely, it is possible to observe a lesson where the teaching is less than satisfactory and the attitude of the learners may be only satisfactory or poor, but the standard of achievement of either kind could be 1/2. Various sets of circumstances could cause this to occur, for example a school could contain pupils of very high ability but the teaching and learning could nevertheless be of poor quality.

External observers of teaching, whose life's work it is to make evidence-based judgements on quality of learning and teaching, are struck frequently by the inability of teachers to evaluate realistically their own competence and skills. Outstanding and good teachers are frequently astonished at having their lessons so described. Similarly, teachers who need to extend the challenge of the lesson or improve its structure are equally surprised to be confronted with these features.

Surgeons improve by observing other surgeons; so do a host of other professions. In that spirit, teachers do improve by observing other teachers and by being observed. The major platform of school self-improvement will be a culture of lesson observation. This will have a by-product of reducing the stress of observation by inspectors when the time arrives for their visit.

The evaluation criteria by which an observer can judge the quality of teaching and learning are well-tried, sound, clear and obvious. Using the competence of the learners in reading, writing, numeracy, oracy and listening to provide evidence for the quality of learning is not surprising. But all the features of the class, clearly presented and fairly judged, are only the outward and visible signs of grace. At the core of teaching and learning there is some mystery just as, after the factors leading to a good marriage have been analysed, the centre of it still remains a mystery. The Framework might regard this as heretical and the inspectors will not be concerned with the mystery at the heart of teaching. But every teacher knows, and all observers who still remember the daily business of teaching know, that all the analysis in the world will not be able to reduce teaching to a purely analytical process. Moreover, the quality of teaching and learning is linked to many other aspects – resources and accommodation for example. The Framework deals with such aspects too.

Each subject of the curriculum is specifically addressed in Section 4 of the Framework guidance, and within each subject the quality of teaching and the quality of learning is described. Consequently a school's internal review can be focused through the subject-specific paragraphs of the Framework on the quality of teaching and the quality of learning. Three methods of conducting an internal review are given below.

Similarly, assessment is vital in its ability to help a child progress to the next stage of learning. Recording and reporting are important in motivating pupils and harnessing parents' support in children's learning. As discussed in Chapter 4, there is a big move in many schools to monitor the progress of children through YELLIS (Year Eleven Information System), ALIS (A Level Information System) and other such programmes. These programmes can be very helpful to teachers in assessing 'value added' progress of pupils, even though inspectors will concentrate on SATS results and public examination results. If inspection is a catalyst to help a school on its continuing journey of self-improvement; if teaching and learning can only be improved by improving in detail, then now is an ideal moment to use devolved GEST (Grant for Education Support and Training) budgets to enable classroom observation to grow as a culture and as a practice that can help teachers, like surgeons, watch each other in order to improve.

Methods of internal review

Method 1   classroom observation

Teaching is difficult. The observation of teaching is difficult. It is manageable and effective if some basic rules are applied.

When classroom observation is being undertaken by colleagues in the school, *negotiation* at the beginning of the process is crucial. The observer teacher needs to negotiate with the teacher to be observed on which class is to be observed, the purpose of the observation and the focus. The preparation before the lesson is observed will need to include a mutual understanding of the *purpose* of the observation. The purpose could be to watch the same class with a number of different teachers in order to observe and judge the management of behaviour of the class. The purpose, on the other hand, might be to observe the quality of learning for many different classes in one subject area. Agreement on the purpose will lead the observed and the observer to discuss the *focus*. In the first example, that of the management of behaviour, an observer and observed might agree to focus on the way in which the junctions of the lessons (beginning, end, change of activity, change from listening to writing) affect the behaviour of children and its management. In the second example, where the purpose is to observe the quality of learning in one subject area, the department could agree that the focus would be concentration, attitude to tasks set, ability to listen to didactic teaching and ability to listen to instructions.

The purpose of the observation will also determine the *model* of observation. There are many models, but three well-tried ones are shown in Figure 5.1.

Figure 5.1 *Three models of observation*

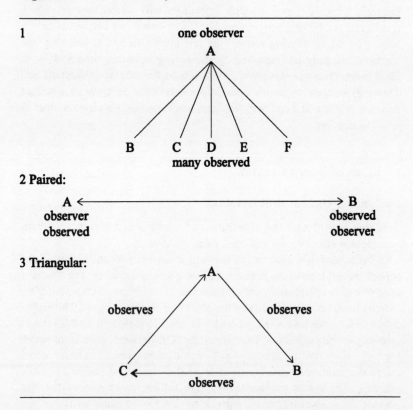

If the school wants to observe one class of children and the management of its behaviour with many teachers, the first model of one observer to many observed is appropriate. Where a Newly Qualified Teacher (NQT) is being observed as part of his/her assessment, a paired model might be useful. The mentor or head of department watches the NQT and then the NQT watches the mentor or head of department in order to observe a more experienced practitioner.

Where a department wants to examine the quality of learning, the triangle works well as it reduces the chances of colluding in the judgement reached.

The preparation includes:

Negotiation	*Focus*
of time and class	of observation
Purpose	*Model*
of observation	agreed to fit purpose

It needs also to include agreement on *ground rules*. The ground rules for observation can be agreed by reference to the school as a whole or to smaller groups, such as a department or year team. There needs to be agreement on: (a) to whom does the information belong once the observation has occurred; (b) the observer's undertaking not to discuss the observation beyond an agreed group or beyond the observed; and (c) the role of the observer – is it to be fly-on-the-wall or interventionist?

A schedule with *evaluation criteria* needs to be agreed. Some LEAs have observation schedules, some schools develop their own and some use OFSTED's schedule, while often focusing only on certain evaluation criteria.

Once the *observation* has taken place, the *debriefing* of the observed by the observer should be arranged as soon as practically possible. The *debriefing* can lead to agreed *outcomes*, and possibly an agreed future observation. For example, during the debrief the observed and the observer might agree to try a new method of working, or of differentiating work between groups of children, which had not been tried before. The observed then asks the observer to watch the same class in four weeks' time to observe what effect the new technique has had.

Classroom observation is a main plank in improvement for the quality of teaching and learning. It is vital to follow the processes discussed above if it is to be a successful and not a threatening experience.

Method 2 sampling children's work

The sampling and reading of children's work has always been a major part of a full HMI inspection. It will continue to be part of an OFSTED inspection. Hitherto, not all schools have used sampling as a regular method of monitoring and evaluating the quality of teaching and of learning.

A method of sampling by HMI was to ask for all the work of six children in every year group. In each year group, the children would represent two of above-average ability, two of average ability and two of below-average ability; preferably a boy and a girl in each of the three categories. It was customary for the full inspection team to read through all the written work of the six children and make judgements on the quality of that work, as well as the way in which it had been marked by the teachers. The registered inspection teams will no doubt adopt a similar method. Some schools already regularly do this themselves. They are monitoring and evaluating in the quality of learning:

- written skills
- presentation
- numeracy
- patterns found
- application of what has been learned
- progress made in knowledge and understanding

In the quality of teaching, by examining the work set, they are monitoring and evaluating:

- expectations
- appropriate homework regularly given
- challenge and differentiation

Through the marking they can also examine:

- consistency
- accuracy
- helpful nature of marking and follow-up
- focus of marking

Just as a school can sample work, so can a department, a head of department or a post-holder. A department or curriculum area may have a series of meetings in a year where different year groups for that subject have their work collected in and read against agreed evaluation criteria. The aspect studied could be the consistency of the marking policy, or it might be the range of written material demanded, or whether the more able pupils have been given sufficiently challenging work to do.

Method 3   a transect

The second method outlined was a broad sampling: a dipstick of written work. The third model is much more like making a transect study: a smaller evaluation in scope, but deeper.

For example, it is possible to take the programme of one class for one term in one subject. All the documentation for that term's programme should be read first. This should include the programme of study, the curriculum plan/scheme of work, the detailed plan, the forecast book, the lesson notes and any retrospective comments on either forecast book or lesson notes. The next step is to examine the children's written work for that subject for that term and to look at the assessment and the marking of the written work.

The teacher should then be interviewed to discuss all the aspects which have emerged from the study and his or her permission should be sought to discuss with a few of the pupils their written work and their view of their progress in that term.

It is possible of course to observe a lesson of this class, but this third method looks primarily at all the written evidence. In examining the written evidence, a reviewer will want to link goals to achievements to assess whether or not time is managed efficiently, the content is appropriate, standards of achievement are good and differentiation is achieved. In addition the reviewer will look for evidence, that homework has been completed regularly, of the learners' level of independence and willingness to tackle new areas, of the learner's perseverance and that they understand their work.

Review of evidence and criteria

Having looked at three methods of structuring a review, it is necessary next to examine the evidence for the *quality of learning*.

1 Observe lessons to evaluate what progress is made in them: progress in knowledge, understanding and skills.

2 Observe lessons to evaluate the pupils' competence as learners in:

- reading
- writing
- numeracy
- oracy

- establishing patterns
- posing questions
- solving problems
- taking decisions

- information seeking   – clear understanding of
       purpose of the task

3 Observe lessons to evaluate the ability of pupils to work in different contexts and to organize resources appropriately.

4 Observe lessons to evaluate pupils' ability to:

- enjoy work
- commit themselves
  to tasks
- respond to
  challenges
- concentrate
- co-operate
- persevere

– sustain a good
  pace of work
– come prepared
  for work
– evaluate realistically
  their own work
  so as to be confident
  about themselves as learners

5 Interview pupils to evaluate the same characteristics as 4.

6 Interview teachers to evaluate the same characteristics as 4.

7 Sample written work to see evidence of commitment to work, enjoyment of work, perseverance, independence as learners.

8 Sample written work to find evidence of competence as learners in: writing, numeracy, information seeking and establishing patterns.

9 Examine evidence of assessments and examination results. Evaluate progress made in understanding, skills and competence.

10 Examine pupils' written work to establish evidence of progress made in understanding, skills and competence.

11 Discussion with teachers for their views on the particular features associated with pupils with SEN which affect their capacity to learn.

For the *quality of teaching*, the person examining the evidence will need to:

1 Look at the curriculum planning, the programmes of study, the forecast books and lesson plans, and see:
   – Were there clear goals for the lesson?
   – Does an individual lesson fit in a sequence?
   – Does the programme of study comply with the National Curriculum?
   – Is the content suitable?

2 Look at the curriculum documentation and planning and see:
   – if they set a time framework for the programme
   – if there is evidence of differentiation

- if a variety of teaching techniques are being used and whether they are appropriate to the purpose of the lesson;
- if a range of learning activities is being used;
- if resources are built into the planning;
- if assessment is built into the planning;
- if pupils are taught in appropriate groupings.

3 Observe a lesson to evaluate if the:
- goals are met;
- NC is complied with, where appropriate;
- lesson fits into an understandable sequence;
- teacher has command of the content;
- lesson is well-timed and has a good pace.

4 Observe a lesson to evaluate if:
- there is an appropriate level of challenge in the work for all, including the most able and the least able;
- there are a variety of techniques of teaching;
- there are a variety of learning activities;
- there are opportunities for pupils to demonstrate choice and responsibility.

5 Observe a lesson to evaluate if:
- differentiation is achieved;
- SEN is addressed;
- language needs are addressed;
- resources are available as needed;
- organizational strategies are effective.

6 Observe a lesson to examine:
- the quality of relationships between teacher and children;
- the motivation engendered;
- the control by the teacher;
- evidence of praise/celebrating success;
- displaying children's work;
- classroom routines;
- appropriate time given to all pupils;
- participation by all;
- whether expectations of pupils by teachers are sufficiently high;
- quality of teacher's discussion and interaction with individuals about their work.

7 Interview a pupil or pupils to examine all points set out in 5 above.

8 Interview the teacher to examine evidence of all points set out in 6 above.

9 Observe a class to look at:
- how resources are organized and used (include everything from displays to visual aids to equipment);
- how groupings are organized;
- how assessment is used as a vehicle of teaching;
- the work of statemented children;
- the role of support teachers/specialists;
- the evidence of the school's equal opportunities policy being implemented.

10 Sample children's work to assess:
- if the homework is appropriate, regularly set and regularly completed;
- if it conforms to the homework policy;
- if the marking is consistent, helpful and responsive.

11 Talk to appropriate teachers to establish if there are arrangements to improve the quality of teaching through observation and INSET.
Examine the evidence of the effect of these on the quality of teaching. What evidence is there of changing practice in teaching and enhanced opportunities for pupils?

12 Observe a lesson to examine:
- the quality of explanation;
- the quality of questioning;
- the quality of discussion or interaction;
- whether sufficient ground has been covered in the lesson;
- whether the lesson is drawn together at the end by summarizing what is important.

13 Interview a teacher to discuss what the teacher's view of the pupils' capabilities is. Compare this view with the standards achieved, either by sampling work or observing a lesson.

14 Look at the accommodation of the class/department. Is it appropriate for the size of class and the activities needed? Is it a stimulating environment for teaching and learning? Is the furniture and space arranged helpfully for learning and teaching?

Table 5.1 *Quality of learning and quality of teaching*

What School can do for Internal Review		What Inspectors can do	Fwk Ref
For Whole School	For Department/ Curriculum/Area		
Observe lessons to evaluate progress made in lessons: gains in knowledge, understanding and skills	Observe lessons of department to evaluate progress made in lessons: gains in knowledge, understanding and skills	Inspect lessons to evaluate progress made: gains in knowledge, understanding and skills Inspect using schedule and putting grades 1-5	3.2
Observe lessons to evaluate pupils' competence as learners, eg reading, oracy etc	Observe lessons of department to evaluate pupils' competence as learners	Inspect lessons to evaluate competence as learners across school, across years and within department Inspect using schedule and putting grades 1-5	3.2
Observe lessons to evaluate pupils' ability to work in different contexts and organize resources	Observe lessons of department to evaluate pupils' ability to work in different contexts and organize resources	Inspect lessons to evaluate pupils' ability to work in different contexts and organize resources Inspect using schedule and putting grades 1-5	3.2
Observe lessons to evaluate learners' attitudes to work	Observe lessons of department to evaluate learners' attitudes to work	Inspect lessons to evaluate learners' attitudes to work Inspect using schedule and putting grades 1-5	3.2
Interview pupils to evaluate attitudes to work	Interview pupils in that subject to evaluate learners' attitudes to work	Interview pupils in lessons and out of lessons to evaluate learners' attitudes to work	3.2

Table 5.1   continued

What School can do for Internal Review		What Inspectors can do	Fwk Ref
For Whole School	**For Department/ Curriculum/Area**		
Interview colleague teachers to evaluate learners' attitudes to work	Interview teachers in department to evaluate learners' attitudes to work	Interview teachers in lesson context and out of it, to evaluate learners' attitudes to work	3.2
Sample written work for evidence of pupils' attitudes to work	Sample written work in department for evidence of pupils' attitudes to work	Sample pupils' written work for evidence of pupils' attitudes to work, both in lessons and in whole-team sampling across school	3.2
Sample written work for evidence of competence as learners, eg writing and establishing patterns	Sample written work in department for evidence of competence as learners, eg writing and establishing patterns	Sample written work for evidence of pupils' competence as learners, both in lessons and in whole-team sampling across school	3.2
Examine assessment results and examination results for evidence of progress	Examine assessment results and examination results in department for evidence of progress	Inspect assessment results and examination results for evidence of progress	3.2
	Look at curriculum planning, POS etc for goals, planning, NC, content etc	Inspect curriculum planning, POS etc for goals, planning etc	7.1
	Look at curriculum documentation and planning for timing, differentiation, variety, resources, assessment and groupings	Inspect curriculum documentation and planning for timing, differentiation, variety, resources, assessment and groupings	7.1

Table 5.1   continued

What School can do for Internal Review		What Inspectors can do	Fwk Ref
For Whole School	**For Department/ Curriculum/Area**		
Observe lessons for goals, NC, sequence, timing and content	Observe lessons of department for goals, NC, sequence, timing and content	Inspect lessons to evaluate goals, NC, sequence, timing and content Inspect using schedule and putting grades 1-5	7.1
Observe lessons for challenge of work, variety of teaching styles, activities, and learner choice and responsibility	Observe lessons of department for challenge of work, variety of teaching styles, activities, and learner choice and responsibility	Inspect lessons for challenge of work, variety of teaching styles, activities, and learner choice and responsibility	7.1
Observe lessons for differentiation, SEN, language, resources and organization	Observe lessons of department for differentiation, SEN, language, resources and organization	Inspect lessons for differentiation, SEN, language, resources and organization	7.1
Observe lessons to evaluate quality of relationships and attitudes of teachers	Observe lessons of department for quality of relationships and attitudes of teachers	Inspect lessons for quality of relationships and attitudes of teachers	7.1
Interview pupils to evaluate quality of relationships etc	Interview pupils in subject area to evaluate quality of relationships etc	Interview pupils, in lessons and out of lessons, to evaluate quality of relationships etc	7.1
Interview teachers to evaluate quality of relationships and attitudes of teachers	Interview teachers in subject area to evaluate quality of relationships and attitudes of teachers	Interview teachers in lesson context and out of lessons, to evaluate quality of relationships and attitudes of teachers	7.1

Table 5.1   continued

What School can do for Internal Review		What Inspectors can do	Fwk Ref
For Whole School	**For Department/ Curriculum/Area**		
Observe classes to evaluate resources, groupings, assessment, role of support teachers, EO and work of statemented children	Observe classes in the department to evaluate resources, groupings, assessment, role of S teachers, EO and work of statemented children	Inspect classes to evaluate resources, groupings, assessment, role of S teachers, EO and work of statemented children Inspect classes using schedule and putting grades 1-5	7.1 7.6 (ii)
Sample children's work for homework and marking	Examine children's work in subject area for homework and marking	Inspects children's work for homework and marking Inspect it in lessons and whole-team sampling	7.1
Observe lessons for quality of questioning etc	Observe lessons in department for quality of questioning etc	Inspect lessons for quality of questioning etc Inspect using schedule and giving grades 1-5	7.1
Interview teachers to discuss teachers' views of pupils' capabilities Compare with standards achieved	Interview teachers in department to discuss teachers' views of pupils' capabilities Compare with standards achieved	Interview teachers to discuss teachers' views of pupils' capabilities Compare with standards achieved	7.1
Look at accommodation Is it helpful for teaching and learning?	Look at accommodation in department Is it helpful for teaching and learning?	Inspect accommodation in schoool Is it helpful for teaching and learning?	7.1 7.6 (iii)

Table 5.2 *OFSTED proforma for lesson observation*

Complete for each lesson or part lesson

DFE SCHOOL NO:_____

SUBJECT/ACTIVITY: ABILITY: Upper Middle Lower Mixed NC YEAR GROUP(s): NOR: PRESENT- B: G: ALL: INSPECTOR: SPECIALIST: Y/N INSPECTOR PRESENT FOR: minutes	
CONTENT OF LESSON (referring to NC PoS and/or ATs where appropriate):	
STANDARDS OF ACHIEVEMENT in relation to national norms: Grade [1]	
STANDARDS OF ACHIEVEMENT in relation to pupils' capabilities: Grade [1]	
QUALITY OF LEARNING: Grade [2]	
QUALITY OF TEACHING: Grade [2]	
CONTRIBUTION TO ACHIEVEMENTS IN OTHER AREAS:	

CONTRIBUTORY FACTORS: Comment on any marked effects of:
 	
       Support Staff: Resources: Accommodation:
Positive:
 	
Negative:
 	
                        OVERALL LESSON GRADE	

[1] Grades: 1 high; 2 above average; 3 average; 4 below average; 5 low.
[2] Grades: 1 very good; 2 good; 3 satisfactory; 4 unsatisfactory; 5 poor.

Table 5.3 *OFSTED proforma for observation of work other than in lessons[1]*

To be used for assemblies (Code AS), examination of individual (I) or groups (G) of pupils and their work, extra-curricular (E) activities, registration periods (R), and any observations of work (O) other than in lessons.

ACTIVITY CODE

YEAR(S):   NUMBER OF PUPILS: NUMBER AND TYPE OF STAFF INVOLVED:

Context:

Inspection evidence and evaluation:

Grade*

*Grades: 1 very good; 2 good; 3 satisfactory; 4 unsatisfactory; 5 poor.

[1]Print on reverse of proforma for lesson observation
© DfE, OFSTED (August 1993)

Chapter 6
The Curriculum
Framework References 7.3(i), 7.3(ii) and 7.4

The curriculum is at the heart of every school, and this chapter examines various aspects of curriculum provision such as whole-school content; organization and planning; cross-curricular themes; skills and dimensions; equality of opportunity; provision for pupils with special educational needs; personal and social education; the pre-vocational curriculum and extra-curricular activities. It also provides checklists and methods to review each aspect of curriculum provision.

Content, organization and planning

According to the Framework for the Inspection of Schools, 'the school's curriculum is judged by the extent to which it contributes to the achievement of high standards, reflects the aims of the school, is broad and balanced, complies with statutory requirements, has a content which is appropriate to pupils' attainments and abilities, prepares pupils for adult life, is organized effectively and is enhanced by extra-curricular activities.' This is underpinned by further criteria under the headings of Equality of Opportunity and Provision for Pupils with Special Educational Needs (SEN), which has its own specific section (7.4).

The school's curriculum documentation should provide evidence on which the inspectors can make a preliminary judgement on how far the school meets these criteria, but it should also enable them to arrive at a firm judgement on the quality of curriculum provision. After that, inspection teams will need to compare the school's documentation with practice.

OFSTED would expect a school's curriculum documentation to include the following:

- the governing body's curriculum policy with a statement of aims, objectives and values;
- curriculum plans, schemes of work and timetables;
- agreed RE syllabus where applicable;
- curriculum audit and priorities written in the school development plan;
- the governing body's policies for sex education (and other curricular responsibilities);
- the timetable and organization of the curriculum, including the arrangement and composition of teaching groups;
- school assessment policy and guidelines, and arrangements for National Curriculum assessment and external examinations;
- specific policy for equality of opportunity;
- provision for pupils with Special Educational Needs;
- whole curriculum planning including cross-curricular themes, skills and dimensions;
- where applicable, pre-vocational education, including careers education and provision for work experience;
- personal and social education;
- extra-curricular opportunities;
- where applicable, the nature and contribution of homework;
- where relevant, specific provision for under-fives.

Before creating or scrutinizing specific curriculum documentation, the school needs to be sure that the curriculum actually offered reflects the overall aims and purposes of the school and the curriculum statement, accepting of course statutory requirements. The curriculum includes not only the formal programme of lessons but also those sections which produce the school's ethos, such as the quality of relationships, the concern for equality of opportunity, the values exemplified in how the curriculum is organized, managed and taught and the nature and support for extra-curricular activities. Section 1 of the Education Reform Act of 1988 places a statutory responsibility upon schools to provide a broad and balanced curriculum which 'promotes the spiritual, moral, cultural, mental and physical development of pupils of the school and of society' and 'prepares pupils for the opportunities, responsibilities and experiences of adult life'.

The National Curriculum alone will not provide the necessary breadth and balance, but the ten subjects specified, together with religious education from the 'basic curriculum', will be augmented by additional subjects, a range of cross-curricular elements, personal and social education (and sex education, where the governing body has so determined) and extra-curricular activities.

A school's curriculum should aim to be broad by bringing *all* pupils into contact with an agreed range of areas of learning and experience, and it should also be balanced in that it offers the adequate development of each area. The curriculum for each year group should be analysed in terms of curricular objectives within and outside the National Curriculum. The time allocated to different parts of the curriculum will also need to be given its own rationale which may include allocations across a week, a year and key stages.

Figure 6.1 *Curriculum consistency*

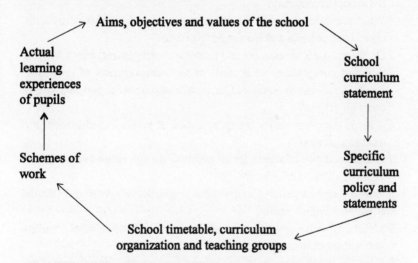

As well as breadth and balance, schools should be offering a relevant curriculum which incorporates continuity and progression in the acquisition of knowledge and understanding. This will include the monitoring of the continuity between the preceding key stage and the succeeding key stage, as well as progression within the key stage itself. Similarly, the relevance and appropriateness of pupils' learning will need to be checked against current policies and actual learning experiences and outcomes. Curriculum documentation should also reflect a concern for the equality of access for all pupils to the full range of educational experiences provided and the rationale behind the arrangements for grouping pupils. The whole curriculum as defined and described by the school should be consistent (see Figure 6.1) and the gap between policy and practice monitored and reviewed.

Checklist for whole-school curriculum review

1 Does the school have a whole curriculum policy? Does it support the achievements of the aims of the school?
2 In what ways is the curriculum organized to achieve the school's aims, objectives and values?
3 How have staff and governors been involved in drawing up curriculum aims, objectives and policies and how are these disseminated through the school community?
4 What provision is made for the monitoring and evaluation of aims, objectives, policies and learning experiences?
5 Do the school's assessment and recording arrangements result in accurate and comprehensive records of the achievements of individual pupils in relation to National Curriculum attainment targets and against other objectives?
6 What is the rationale for the organization of pupils into classroom and teaching groups?
7 Is there equality of access for all pupils to the full range of experiences included in the curriculum?
8 How do agreed policies address the linguistic, religious and cultural experiences of all pupils?
9 Is there effective progression and continuity within the whole curriculum and specific curriculum areas?
10 Does the curriculum fully implement the statutory provisions of the National Curriculum and the basic curriculum? What subjects are provided in addition to the basic curriculum?
11 Is there an appropriate and effective allocation of time to all learning experiences? What criteria are used to decide time allocations?

(A summary of curriculum review appears in Table 6.3, p.102)

Cross-curricular themes, skills and dimensions

The inspector's report will include an evaluation of the provision made for cross-curricular elements in terms of meeting the needs of all pupils and the requirements of Section 1 of the Education Reform Act. The National Curriculum Council has identified and defined five cross-curricular themes that are an essential part of the whole curriculum:

1 Economic and industrial understanding, covering such aspects of industry and the economy as business, commerce, finance and consumer affairs and pupils' direct experience of industry and the world of work.

2 Careers education and guidance, including the development of self-awareness and access to individual guidance and up to date sources of information about educational, vocational, training and careers opportunities.

3 Health education, which covers sex education, family life education, use and misuse of substances, safety, health-related exercise, nutrition, personal hygiene and the effects of various environments upon health.

4 Education for citizenship, which aims to establish the importance of positive, participative citizenship and provide the motivation to join in and to help pupils acquire and understand essential information on which to base the development of their skills, values and attitudes towards citizenship.

5 Environmental education, which is concerned with promoting positive and responsible attitudes towards the environment. It aims to increase pupils' knowledge and understanding of the processes by which environments are shaped, to enable them to recognize both the quality and vulnerability of different environments, and to help them identify opportunities for protecting and managing the environment.

It is open to schools to decide how these themes are encompassed within the whole curriculum, but they should appear in a coherent and planned manner throughout the curriculum in a form which ensures continuity and progression. This is a curriculum 'mapping' exercise, and schools should review their existing provision of cross-curricular themes, identify the gaps and make appropriate provision. There are many different strategies that schools can use and school policy and planning in this area should consider the following:

1 Auditing and mapping cross-curriculum provision through subjects. Particular aspects of those themes could be the major responsibility of certain subject areas and be represented in their schemes of work, while accepting that all subjects have some connection to the five themes. Examples would be:

- Science: economic and industrial understanding
- Physical Education: health education
- Geography: environmental education; economic and industrial understanding

- History: citizenship; economic and industrial understanding; health education
- Technology: careers education; economic and industrial understanding; environmental education

However, all subjects should have policy statements on their particular contribution to the delivery of these cross-curricular themes, and this should be reflected in their curriculum planning and schemes of work.

2 Separate and clearly identifiable free-standing courses with units of study which deliver specific elements of those themes, eg personal and social educational units, tutorial programmes, careers education.

3 Specific themes which can be included in a topic approach to learning and be built in on a planned basis across a number of subjects.

4 Periodic suspension of the school timetable to concentrate on a particular theme for a day or a week, eg:

- a Healthy Eating Day
- an Industry Day/ work simulations

- a careers exhibition
- a mock election day

5 Permeating the whole curriculum through the demonstration and exemplification of themes in the life of the educational community, eg:

- assemblies
- clubs and societies

- community and charity work
- displays and exhibitions

Schools should be able to write down and articulate their strategies for delivering these cross-curricular themes and inspectors will look for evidence of planned provision, classroom delivery and whole-school pupil experiences.

Similarly, schools will want to demonstrate that cross-curricular *skills* are developed across the curriculum in a measured and planned way. For particular skills identified by the National Curriculum Council see Chapter 4, page 61.

All these skills are transferable, mainly independent of context and can be developed in different contexts across the whole curriculum. Schools should review those contexts and be able to describe when and how these particular skills are practised, the means of continuity and progression and the contribution of specific curriculum areas to their development.

Cross-curricular *dimensions*, such as equality of opportunity and provision for pupils with Special Educational Needs, are given their own specific sections in the inspection schedule with identified criteria and evidence, and will be examined in more detail later in this chapter. It is, however, worth reflecting on other dimensions, such as educating pupils for life in a multicultural society by extracting knowledge and understanding of different cultures, languages and faiths, offering positive images and role models from all cultures, and valuing cultural diversity by drawing on pupils' backgrounds and experiences.

In planning the provision and implementation of cross-curricular dimensions, schools need to consider positively ways in which these should underpin and permeate the whole curriculum and be the responsibility of all teachers. Such dimensions help develop pupils' attitudes and understanding, and schemes of work, classroom planning and practice should all demonstrate a recognition that life in a multicultural society is relevant to all pupils, an understanding of the cultural diversity of society, the provision of equal opportunities for pupils irrespective of gender, ability or cultural and ethnic background, and should cater for the special needs of all pupils. The delivery of cross-curricular themes, skills and dimensions needs to be reviewed and audited at the levels of the whole-school policy, subject and course planning, and classroom delivery so that there is a coherent entitlement for all pupils.

Checklist for review

1 Who is responsible for ensuring the development of cross-curricular themes and monitoring their delivery?
2 Does the school have policies for cross-curricular elements? Are they working documents?

3 What strategies are being adopted to ensure the successful development of cross-curricular work?

4 How are learners enabled to see the links between skills and themes being developed across a range of curriculum areas?

5 Is there a curriculum map that demonstrates where cross-curricular themes are being delivered? Are there any gaps?

6 How do cross-curricular dimensions underpin and permeate the whole curriculum?

7 Is there guidance on how day-to-day teaching might contribute to cross-curricular themes, skills and dimensions?

8 Are elements of cross-curricular provision embodied in the work of subjects?

Equality of opportunity (EO)

The commitment to providing equal opportunities for all pupils should permeate every aspect of the curriculum. The OFSTED evaluation criteria refer to the extent to which 'all pupils, irrespective of gender, ability (including giftedness), ethnicity and social circumstance, have access to the curriculum and make the greatest progress possible'. They are also concerned with how far the school 'meets the requirements of the Sex Discrimination Act (1975) and the Race Relations Act (1976)'. This means ensuring that all pupils have access to the curriculum and the National Curriculum, which itself makes a common curriculum for all pupils apart from a small minority of exceptional cases.

However, there are other barriers which stand in the way of access to the curriculum. Schools need to monitor and review the influence of gender and ethnicity on pupil grouping arrangements and subject choices. Examination and assessment results should be explored for considerable differences between the achievement of specific groups of pupils.

The quality of the school's approach to, and planning for, equal opportunities will be seen from an examination of specific documentation. Fundamentally, this ought to be analysed from the school's policy statements referring to different aspects of equal opportunity, curriculum content and access, pupil grouping arrangements, and the extent and location of any direct teaching about equal opportunity issues. However, these policies have to be seen in operation in the curriculum and life of the school, and this is an issue of teaching and learning. Subject areas and individual teachers need to demonstrate through their management, planning and teaching that they have appreciated how factors such as ethnicity, gender and social circumstance affect learning. Schemes of work should refer to the quality and range of curriculum content and teaching strategies for equal opportunities. The observation of learning will provide evidence of the extent to which equal demands are made on ethnic and gender groups, the choice of materials, the extent of pupils' knowledge and understanding about the issues, and the teachers' ability to establish appropriate working groups of pupils and to avoid stereotyping, especially in expectations of achievement. Similarly, discussions with pupils will provide evidence on the extent and value of any curriculum work on equal opportunities and how the school provides for the needs of individuals and groups, and their attitudes to differences in race, culture and gender.

The basic issue under review is the school's ability to foster a climate in which equality of opportunity is supported by policies and practices to which the whole school subscribes and in which positive attitudes to gender equality, cultural diversity and special needs of all kinds are actively promoted, monitored and reviewed.

Checklist for review (EO)

1 To what extent are the principles of entitlement, equality of access and opportunity part of *explicit* curriculum policies?

2 Are schemes of work consistent with whole-school policy statements relating to equality of opportunity?

3 Do teachers have adequate resources and support to promote equal opportunities teaching?

4 To what extent do teaching and material resources reflect the gender, cultural and ethnic makeup of the pupils?

5 What are the specific support arrangements for individuals and different groups? What use is made of support arrangements and other personnel under Section 11 of the Local Government Act?

6 To what extent is adequate provision made for pupils whose home language is not English?

7 How effectively are policies and intentions communicated to and accepted by staff, pupils, governors and parents?

8 Does the school have active monitoring systems with reference to how different groups perform in terms of assessment and examination

results, leavers' destinations, appropriate proportion of groups reflected in higher activity teaching groups, groups representing the school and participation in extra-curricular activities?

Provision for pupils with special educational needs (SEN)

SEN provision is judged according to OFSTED criteria by the extent to which the school enables pupils with Special Educational Needs 'to make the greatest progress possible, and to gain access to a broad and balanced curriculum which includes the National Curriculum (unless modified or disapplied), religious education and other curricular provisions.'

School policies, practices and procedures should be evaluated on how these pupils are identified and monitored, how access to the curriculum is maximized and how the highest possible standards are achieved in all areas of development.

The starting point will obviously be the school's policy on special needs, including identifying, planning, assessing, monitoring and evaluating the implementation of special needs provision. There should be some analysis on how the policy is drawn up and reviewed by staff and governors in consultation with the wider community. In both mainstream and special schools, good practice is most likely to be advanced when all members of staff are committed to the same aims: providing a broad, balanced, relevant and differentiated curriculum, and raising standards for each of the pupils they teach. This needs to be followed by an examination of schemes of work, individual work programmes, samples of pupils' records and standards, and resource provision. Critical questions need to be asked about assessment and recording, and access to all areas of the curriculum, including the National Curriculum, unless modification and disapplication is specified in individual statements. The school should also have plans for catering for exceptionally able students through extension (allowing pupils to progress faster to higher order skills) and enrichment (broadening experiences within levels).

The effectiveness of curricular provision should be judged on whether practices meet the range of needs found in the pupil group, and whether grouping and support systems are appropriate.

The school should have a clear rationale as to why and how pupils with SEN are grouped, integrated into mainstream classes or withdrawn for individual work and be able to provide an outline of the organizational issues involved.

An analysis of the standards obtained by pupils with SEN through better observation and sampling of pupils' work will enable a judgement to be made as to whether there are significant gains in knowledge and skills, and the development of physical and interpersonal skills for the individual learners concerned. High expectations of pupils should be an important factor in this judgement.

An important factor in the education provision for pupils with SEN are the contributions from support teachers, support assistants and educational psychologists, and the school needs to demonstrate that this support is planned systematically and coherently, and its effectiveness evaluated against the range of needs. Where there are designated special needs teachers in mainstream schools there should be documented guidance in these curriculum areas where guidance is offered for integrated classes, eg strategies for developing oracy, literacy and numeracy, and advice on differentiation, classroom management and resource organization.

Schools should make sure that special needs resourcing is clearly identified as part of the budget and that professional and material resources are effectively deployed into the life and work of the school. Complete lists of resources, storage and access are important issues in underpinning learning in mainstream classes as well as individual programmes.

Checklist for review (SEN)

1 How are Special Educational Needs defined? What is the process for assessing special learning needs?
2 Is special needs provision based upon an appropriate school policy? How was this policy arrived at and how is it monitored and evaluated?
3 Are there clear procedures and guidelines for all teaching staff concerning special needs provision? Do all staff know which pupils have special educational needs and how best to meet these needs?
4 Is a delegated member of staff responsible for co-ordinating a school-wide SEN policy?
5 Do curriculum areas/departments have specific policies within the context of the whole-school policy?
6 To what extent are special needs pupils integrated into mainstream? If taught separately or withdrawn, what is the rationale for this and what are the educational and social outcomes?

7 Do classroom strategies indicate that sufficient thought has been given to the identification and inclusion of pupils with special educational needs?

8 What standards are obtained by pupils with special educational needs? How is progression monitored?

9 How are pupils of all abilities encouraged to recognize and celebrate their successes?

10 What is the quality of accommodation and resourcing? How effective is the use of support staff?

11 How does the school encourage a sharing of expertise about SEN among all members of staff? What training is available to staff?

Personal and social education

Of course the whole curriculum contributes to the personal and social education of all pupils and all schools are charged with preparing young people to take their place in a wide range of roles in adult life. The school also has a responsibility to educate individuals to be able to think and act for themselves with an acceptable set of personal qualities and values which will meet the wider demands of adult life. This goes beyond the National Curriculum, religious education, additional subjects and cross-curricular elements, and encompasses the quality of relationships, how the curriculum is managed and assessed, its organization and the teaching and learning methods deployed. This unique combination of factors which makes up the *ethos* of a school – aims, attributes, values and procedures – all make an important contribution to personal and social education in schools. Within the curriculum as a whole and apart from assemblies, tutor periods and social education programmes, teachers and schools will need to be able to demonstrate their concern with the personal development of individual pupils, with their welfare, and with helping them to gain satisfaction and maximum benefit from their experiences in school.

Checklist for review

1 Is there a specific policy statement on personal and social education? How is the policy shared with parents and governors?

2 How are the aims and objectives reflected in the working practice of the school?

3 How is the personal and social education of pupils planned across the curriculum?
4 What monitoring system exists within the delivery of personal and social education to ensure coherence?
5 What training and staff development have been provided to enable all teachers to deliver the pastoral curriculum?

The pre-vocational curriculum

This can be defined as preparing young people for the world of work and evidence of this is cited in the inspection schedule in the school's programme for careers education, contributions to the curriculum by local industry, work experience arrangements and technical and vocational education provision. Schools have the responsibility to develop in their pupils, progressively throughout the primary and secondary years, the understanding, skills and attributes which provide a sound basis of competence and commitment for their future lives and work. They need to show that there is a commitment to improving pupils' understanding of business, commerce, industry and public services, not only through work experience but also through access to information and planned curriculum activities. Opportunities should be provided for links between local enterprises and the staff and students of the school, together with local business education partnerships. For work experience itself, the school should have a clear set of objectives that demonstrate its integration into the whole curriculum provision, which may include at various stages: work visits, mini enterprise schemes, simulations, the application of industrial processes in the classroom, project work and practical work experience.

Checklist for review

1 What evidence is there of a coherent and carefully planned careers education programme for all pupils?
2 How does the school seek to influence the formation of career aspirations through role models, resource materials, displays, staffing and non-teacher adults in the school?
3 What arrangements exist for work experience? How does this fit into the school curriculum and how is it monitored?

4 What system does the school use for monitoring option and career choices and does this take into account gender, ethnicity, social disadvantage and Special Educational Needs?
5 Does the development of the pre-vocational curriculum involve wide consultation with parents, governors, employers, careers officers, further and higher education establishments, business educational partnerships and the Training and Education Council?

Extra-curricular activities

These form part of the life at every school and take place outside class or lesson time, and extend beyond the formal school day. They need to be taken account of and written down as part of the whole curriculum to reinforce their importance, as they can be seen as a way of projecting many of the values of the school to pupils, parents and the local community. Information required by inspectors will include a list of extra-curricular activities with an indication of the proportion of students in each age range who regularly participate. Schools do need to audit the range and type of extra-curricular opportunities on offer, and this can be done using the following headings:

Sporting   –   Eg teams, individual opportunities, range of provision and access

Artistic   –   Music, drama, dance, art

Practical   –   Craft skills, information technology, mini enterprises

Academic   –   Extension and enrichment of subject knowledge and skills

Social   –   Charity and community work, citizenship activities

Personal   –   Positions of responsibility and further personal development through a choice of activities which may contribute to the record of achievement

Educational visits   –   Theatre, historical sites, museums, fieldwork, business

Residential experiences   –   Outdoor education, visits abroad

The inspectors' report will include an evaluation of the extent to which the curriculum is enhanced by extra-curricular provision and its benefits to pupils, and the following questions should assist schools in reviewing provisions for themselves.

Checklist for review

1 What statistical evidence is there regarding pupil participation rates in extra-curricular activities?
2 What opportunities are there for learners to develop personal talents and interests beyond the normal curriculum? How is teacher time managed to support this?
3 How are pupil contributions in these areas recognized and valued?
4 What access is there to school resources outside the normal working day?
5 In what ways does the school extend pupils' experiences through contact with different cultures?

Methods of reviewing curriculum quality and range

Method 1   whole-school curriculum documentation audit

Is the school's documentation up to date and sufficient? Does it meet statutory requirements? Is it 'owned' by all members of staff? See Table 6.1.

Table 6.1 *Reviewing whole-school curriculum quality and range*

Documentation Required	Needs Creating/ Revising	Lead Person Responsible	Method of Review	Timescale
Curriculum statement				
School development plan				
School timetables (pupil and staff)				
Organization of teaching groups				
Special Education Needs policy				

Table 6.1 continued

Documentation Required	Needs Creating/ Revising	Lead Person Responsible	Method of Review	Timescale
Pre-vocational education				
Planning for cross-curricular elements				
Assessment policy and guidelines for monitoring standards				
Options guidance – for KS4 and post-16				

Method 2   subject/reviewing for consistent documentation

For the inspection of subjects, the general and evaluation criteria set out by OFSTED in each section of the schedule apply to the following aspects:

Standards of achievement.
Quality of learning.
Quality of teaching.
Assessment, recording and reporting.
Curriculum content: subject quality and range; equality of opportunity.
Management and administration.
Resources and their management.
Resources.
Accommodation.

It is therefore essential to keep under review the relationship of subject documentation to whole-school policies and the learning process. Schools will want to establish systems to ensure coherence and consistency for every subject area and this can be achieved through establishing subject handbooks as working documents based on particular section headings.

Subject leaders should use these for audit and review. See the suggested list below.

- Departmental (secondary), subject co-ordination (primary); management and organization, including staff responsibilities
- Aims and objectives linked to the whole-school curriculum statement and general aims
- Schemes of work (demonstrating coverage of the National Curriculum, planning, differentiation, continuity and progression as well as knowledge, skills, concepts, values and attitudes)
- Teaching methods and learning strategies (relating to the quality of learning, quality of teaching and standards of achievement)
- Assessment, recording and reporting (eg marking, collecting evidence, internal moderation, examinations, course work, assessment and reporting documentation – link to whole-school assessment policy)
- Cross-curricular skills, dimensions and themes (link to whole-school policies)
- Extra-curricular provision
- Homework (policy and types of), where applicable
- Equal opportunities (race and gender – link to whole-school policy); Special Needs (including the most able – link to whole-school policy)
- Communication (senior management team (SMT); whole school; governors; parents/community)
- Departmental/subject development plan (annual targets and success criteria)
- Systems of monitoring and review (self-supported evaluation with SMT validating the process and outcomes on a systematic basis)
- Resources and accommodation/departmental environment/health and safety issues

Method 3   reviewing classroom planning and delivery

The crucial issue here is the *match* between whole-school policies, curriculum policies and procedures, and classroom planning and delivery. Schools need to devise some way of illustrating this match between philosophy and practice through schemes of work and other working documents, although it has to be remembered that the ultimate test will be the observation of pupils' learning. The scheme of work should reflect whole-school approaches to teaching and learning and be a practical guide to teaching within the school's curriculum problem.

Scheme of work

A written statement is produced which describes the work plan for pupils within a class or group over a specific period. See Table 6.2.

Table 6.2 *Example of a scheme of work*

Content	Attainment Targets	Method	Cross-Curricular Elements	Special Needs/Diff-erentiation	Equality of Opportunity	Resources
Programme of study (indicate period of time)						

Table 6.3 *The curriculum*

What School can do for Internal Review		What Inspectors can do	Fwk Ref
For Whole School	For Department/ Curriculum/Area		
Check the curriculum statement against OFSTED criteria and evidence Establish how well this is disseminated and understood	Relative subject documentation to whole school curriculum aims and objectives Are they consistent?	Analyse the school's curriculum statement of aims and objectives Match policy to practice	7.3 (i)

Table 6.3 *continued*

What School can do for Internal Review		What Inspectors can do	Fwk Ref
For Whole School	**For Department/ Curriculum/Area**		
Audit the whole curriculum What are the strengths and weaknesses? What are the gaps? What action is needed to fill them? Analyse the use of time across years and key stages	Review how programmes of study, attainment targets and non-statutory guidance are used and the quality of schemes of work and lesson planning	Analyse and evaluate curriculum plans and timetable for breadth, balance, relevance and differentiation across years and key stages, and analyse curriculum continuity Inspect legal compliance with the National Curriculum and RE Compare policy to practice in lessons and discuss with staff and pupils	7.3 (i)
Review pupil groupings in the light of enabling all pupils to reach their full potential Is there a school policy for review and adjustment of groupings?	Review grouping strategies and explain the rationale behind them Sample pupils' work	Inspect and analyse the arrangements and composition of teaching groups – examine the incidence of very large and very small groups and gender balance	7.3 (i)
Review policy statements and audit strategies for delivering cross-curriculum themes, skills and dimension to demonstrate coherence across subjects and the whole curriculum	Review the contribution of the subject to cross-curriculum themes, skills and dimensions Check against whole-school policies	Inspection of the planning and delivery of cross-curriculum themes, skills and dimensions Refer to scheme of work and lesson plans	7.3 (i)

Table 6.3   continued

What School can do for Internal Review		What Inspectors can do	Fwk Ref
For Whole School	For Department/ Curriculum/Area		
Review arrangements for curriculum guidance and the monitoring of takeup of subjects by specific groups of pupils	Review subject guidance to pupils and parents and investigate patterns of takeup in the subject	Investigate access and constraints on pupils' choices and the takeup of subjects in terms of gender, ethnicity and ability	7.3 (i)
Review/create policy for personal and social education and preparation for adult life How coherent and consistent is the delivery of personal and social education? Observe teaching in this area	Review the contribution of the subject/curriculum area to personal and social education Check out against the school policy	Analyse and inspect the methods of planning and delivering personal and social education Interview teachers with responsibility for this area and a cross-section of all teachers	7.3 (i)
Review the school's careers education and work experience arrangements, and contributions to the curriculum by local industry and employers Observe careers teaching where applicable	Review the contribution of the subject/curriculum area to pre-vocational education and its links to TVE where applicable	Analyse and inspect the methods of planning and delivering pre-vocational education Interview teachers with responsibility for this	7.3 (i)

Table 6.3   continued

What School can do for Internal Review		What Inspectors can do	Fwk Ref
For Whole School	**For Department/ Curriculum/Area**		
Review the range, type and extent of extra-curricular provision and its availability to all pupils Secondary: Examine percentage takeups by year groups	Audit the contribution of subjects to extra-curricular activities	Inspect the provision and range of extra-curricular activities and participation levels Observe activities	7.3 (i)
Review/create whole-school strategies for monitoring and evaluating the curriculum, such as lesson observations, subject reviews, assessment checks, development plans and analysis of examination results	Have agreed monitoring and evaluation strategies such as peer observation of teaching and learning, sampling pupils' work, detailed analysis of assessment and examination outcomes	Inspect the school's arrangements and strategies for monitoring and evaluating its curriculum and standard of achievement Interview senior staff and curriculum leaders	7.3 (i)
Review/create whole-school policy on equality of opportunity with reference to gender, ethnicity and social circumstance Check on dissemination and application across the school Analyse data	Review the contribution of the subject/curriculum area to equal opportunities and write this down Check out against whole-school policy	Analyse the school's policy statement for equality of opportunity and inspect its effects on the quality and standard of pupils' work	7.3 (ii)

Table 6.3 continued

What School can do for Internal Review		What Inspectors can do	Fwk Ref
For Whole School	**For Department/ Curriculum/Area**		
Monitor curriculum content across the school and teaching about equal opportunities Analyse data on access	Monitor subject content and investigate access for all pupils to the subject	Inspect lessons regarding curriculum content and access for all pupils Sample pupils' work	7.3 (ii)
Review and monitor pupil grouping arrangements across the whole curriculum in terms of gender, ethnicity and ability	Review and monitor pupil grouping arrangements with reference to gender, ethnicity and ability in the subject area	Inspect lessons for pupil grouping arrangements and the extent to which equal demands are made on each gender and ethnic group	6.3 (ii)
Review and sample resource provision in curriculum areas and the library Monitor Section 11 funding	Review quality and appropriateness of resources in review of subject provision and revise accordingly	Inspect the quality and appropriateness of resources including the use made of Section 11 funding Interview appropriate staff	7.3 (ii)
Monitor procedures used to examine bias in aspects such as success rates and leavers' destinations	Explore National Curriculum assessment results and examinations for consistent differences between achievements of specific groups of pupils	Analyse the nature of the school's intake and key statistics relating to assessment, examination results, exclusions and leavers' destinations	7.3 (ii)

Table 6.3   continued

What School can do for Internal Review		What Inspectors can do	Fwk Ref
For Whole School	**For Department/ Curriculum/Area**		
Review the priority of equal opportunity in the school development plan and the extent and location of any direct teaching about equal opportunities issues	Review documentation and strategies to address equal opportunities issues in the subject curriculum and techniques of monitoring this	Inspect school arrangements and documentation for monitoring and evaluating its equal opportunities policy and and strategies Interview senior staff and curriculum leaders	7.3 (ii)
Review policy for special educational needs and its application across the whole curriculum and subject areas	Review the contribution of the subject to the provision of special educational needs and write this down Check against whole-school policy	Analyse the school's policy statement for special educational needs Interview the special needs post-holder	7.4
Evaluate strategies for regular review of progress and sample pupils' individual work programmes	Evaluate grouping and support systems and the differentiation of learning to match individual needs Do clear strategies exist?	Inspect the extent to which provision and practice meet the range of SEN through lesson observation and samples of pupils' records and statements	7.4
Monitor the coherence of whole-school planning and support and links to other support staff	Evaluate support strategies for the delivery of teaching and learning in specific areas	Investigate pupils with statements and their level of support Interview pupils and support staff	7.4

Table 6.3   continued

What School can do for Internal Review		What Inspectors can do	Fwk Ref
For Whole School	**For Department/ Curriculum/Area**		
Monitor staff awareness of, and commitment to, the special needs policy, together with appropriate expectations Review INSET provision	Review links to special needs department of post holder and links to external agencies	Inspect staffing provision, expertise and qualifications, and INSET, including links to external agencies	7.4
Evaluate the way the school distinguishes between and caters for different kinds of need	Review the ways in which pupils with SEN are grouped, integrated into mainstream classes and withdrawn for individual work	Inspect lessons for the extent, effectiveness and appropriateness of integration within the the school	7.4
Review how professional and material resources are deployed across the school to support special needs Examine specialist accommodation	Evaluate resource provision for special needs pupils	Inspect specialist accommodation and resource provision generally for special needs	7.4

Chapter 7

Pupils' Personal Development and Behaviour

Framework References 5.1, 5.2 and 5.3

Inspectors will make judgements in three areas on pupils' personal development and behaviour : (1) their spiritual, moral, social and cultural development (PSMSCD); (2) behaviour and discipline; and (3) attendance. These are 'output' judgements.

Everyone who works in a school knows that these three areas tell us not only about the quality of the school community but also give clues about each individual's development, and his or her individual aspirations and achievements.

Inspecting and reviewing *attendance* is a relatively simple and fairly mechanical process. Summarizing judgements on *behaviour* is not difficult. It is the gathering together of every inspector's view after days in a school. The views and evidence may be contradictory, but it is not difficult to undertake the process.

The real difficulty is for the school reviewer. It is difficult to be objective; it is hard to make comparisons on behaviour once the teacher has become immersed in one school over a period; it is tempting to colour general perceptions because of singular experiences; it is very difficult to be detached about behaviour when the reviewer is a member of staff who every day manages it in class, in corridors and in many other areas. For example, a pastoral head who spends a disproportionate amount of time on children with bad behaviour may find it hard to be objective. The reviewer needs some hard criteria to work on, and may decide to involve a governor or another outsider in the review processes because of the inherent difficulties in internally reviewing behaviour. The Framework specifically connects high standards of behaviour and effective learning and standards of achievement.

When it comes to *pupils' spiritual, moral, social and cultural development*, even inspectors find this very difficult. Good schools, and self-improving schools, work very hard and successfully at these aspects but have rarely planned them systematically. Since inspectors will examine systematically evidence in these areas, reviewers can take the opportunity to describe what the school is doing and use the opportunity to treat inspection as a catalyst to fill the gaps in their own practice. The August 1993 Framework has expanded its guidance (Part 4) on this from four lines to three pages. It gives specific subject examples. It has also revised the evaluation criteria for the four aspects: spiritual, moral, social and cultural.

The Framework observes particularly that 'The 1992 Act makes separate provision for the inspection of denominational education in those schools where it is provided'. The National Curriculum Council paper on spiritual and moral development notes that there are three areas of school life in which there are opportunities for spiritual and moral development: the ethos of the school, all subjects of the curriculum and collective worship.

To illustrate methods of reviewing the quality of the school as a community, we shall now give a general overview and an individual tracking exercise will be given for each of the three strands (Framework 5.1, 5.2 and 5.3).

Method of internal review (PSMSCD)

A general review: wide-angle lens

1 Read the documentation, starting with the criteria in the schedule. Then read:

– the school's aims   – codes of conduct/
– subject schemes of work   sanctions and rewards

- RE scheme of work
- evidence of arrangements for collective worship
- pupil welfare (primary)
- pastoral guidance and support policy (secondary)
- governors' policy on sex education
- data on extra-curricular activities
- data on community service, charity work, school council noticeboards for evidence of the wider community

for evidence of the extent to which:

- the school has agreed approaches to the ways in which spiritual, moral, social and cultural development should be addressed consistently through all the subjects in the curriculum and through the general life of the school;
- the school's aims promote *spiritual, moral, cultural and social development;*
- collective worship and religious education contribute to spiritual, moral cultural *and social* development of pupils;
- collective worship complies with the law;
- sex education considers moral issues;
- pastoral care helps to develop a moral code;
- the code of conduct impacts on daily life and promotes honesty and consideration for others;
- a wide range of cultures is recognized in written documentation;
- pupils are involved in extra-curricular life;
- the aims of the code of conduct reflect spiritual, moral and social values;
- the curriculum is being widened through participation in a range of cultural activities;
- pupils' interests are being widened by the school.

Inspectors will read the documentation before arriving in the school and during the week of the inspection.

2 Observe:

- lessons
- collective worship
- PSE lessons
- daily life of the school
- school meals
- playgrounds
- buses
- reception of visitors
- school council
- extra-curricular activities

for evidence of:

- general ethos;
- whether curriculum addresses pupils' spiritual, moral and cultural development;
- the quality of relationships in the school; role models provided by the adults in the school;
- opportunities for pupils to express ideas and opinions about religious and moral isues;
- whether the styles of teaching encourage an increasingly mature response to personal experience and social issues;
- opportunities for pupils to develop their own values and to learn to appreciate beliefs and practices of others;
- responsible attitudes to people and property, work, school, the community and the environment;
- opportunities for pupils to take on responsibilities for themselves and others;
- the extent of links and benefits between the school and the wider community;
- concern for the more vulnerable members of the community;
- whether the cultural richness of the immediate and wider community is reflected in the life of the school.

Inspectors will be making such observations during the inspection. In some cases these observations will be part of a wider observation. In others, they will specifically go to an extra-curricular activity, for example, to inspect for evidence in this part of the schedule.

3   Discuss with:

chair(man)	parents
headteacher	some HODs
pupils	some pastoral heads

for evidence of:

- governors' and staff commitment to spiritual, moral, social and cultural development of pupils;
- the extent of the school's contribution to spiritual, moral, social and cultural development through the curriculum and daily life of the school;
- pupils having a clear view of what is expected of them;

- pupils' ability to converse confidently with mutual respect;
- pupils' values, attitudes, behaviour;
- how the school takes account of the religious background of its pupils;
- the parents having clear and regular communication from the school of what is expected of their children;
- the view of the ethos of the school, which all members of the school have and whether, if at all, they would like to change it;
- teachers having a consistent approach in teaching, pastoral care and behaviour policy;
- the headteacher having a clear view of whether aims are being addressed in the daily life of the school and curriculum and the ethos of the school; whether the school has a context and a vocabulary for spiritual, moral, social and cultural development;
- where in the curriculum there are opportunities for spiritual and moral development;
- pupils valuing the experience of collective worship;
- how the school ensures that collective worship promotes the spiritual and moral development of pupils;
- opportunities for personal involvement in a range of interests;
- schools links with a wider community, and views on these;
- opportunities for and quality of pupils' contributions to the school.

Inspectors will be holding such conversations either as specific conversations on this area or as part of another conversation.

It is worth quoting in full the Framework's 'Health Warning' in the amplification of evaluation criteria for pupils' spiritual and moral guidance:

> 'Spiritual, moral, social and cultural development are difficult aspects to inspect. They deal with highly personal issues and inspectors should be aware that some families and cultures would regard detailed discussion of such matters with pupils as offensive intrusion. Inspectors should not allow their personal views to intrude upon discussion or to colour judgements. Especially when a school has a high proportion of ethnic minority pupils representing world faiths other than Christianity, it is important not to confuse culture and religion. It is also important not to confuse ethnicity with particular religious belief.'

Structuring an internal review

Tracking a sample of pupils' SMSCD: zoom lens approach

The April 1993 NCC discussion paper on spiritual and moral development says:

> 'Schools are strongly advised not to attempt to assess pupils' spiritual and moral development. Such an activity could be regarded as intrusive and any judgements made highly subjective. However, schools should evaluate the curriculum and other areas of school life to ensure that appropriate opportunities for spiritual and moral development are being provided.'

In the light of the 'Health Warning' quoted from the Framework in the previous section, and of the NCC paper also quoted here, ask for volunteers. You want a volunteer or volunteers whom you can shadow to collective worship, a PSE lesson, RE lesson, and an extra-curricular activity.

Observe all four. Then hold a discussion with the teachers involved, in order to find evidence:

- that spiritual and moral development is a planned part of the curriculum;
- that pupils have the opportunity to develop their own personal values and morality code, and to learn to appreciate the beliefs and practices of others;
- of the extent and nature of the extra-curricular activities (a pupil might be able to show the reviewer their record of achievements);
- the way lessons help the cultural development of pupils;
- the way lessons help the social development of pupils;
- the opportunities the pupils have to exercise responsibility and show initiative;
- of pupil experiences with charity work and work in the wider community;
- of ways in which collective worship helps cultural and social development;
- ways in which school life helps pupils to understand the structure and processes of society;
- pupils' attitudes to people and property;
- pupils' attitudes towards the more vulnerable members of the community;
- that pupils have a clear idea of what is expected of them;

- that there are opportunities for pupils to express ideas and opinions on spiritual and moral issues;
- that there are attitudes of a shared corporate life and ethos.

Structuring an internal review of behaviour and discipline

A general review: wide-angle lens

1 Read the documentation, including:

- the school's aims
- behaviour policy
- code of conduct, rewards
    and sanctions

- any documentation on
    countering bullying
- summary of Elton's findings
- amplification of criteria
    set out in the Framework

Also examine:

- data on exclusions and referrals
- a sample of pupils' records

for evidence of:

- promotion of good behaviour;
- partnership to promote good behaviour;
- promotion of orderly community;
- promotion of safe, co-operative community;
- promotion of consistent expectations and appropriate strategies.

Inspectors will do the reading of the school documentation before they arrive and during the inspection week.

2 *Observe* a range of activities (in Part 7, page 20 of the Framework might help):

- lessons
- breaktimes
- changeovers
- junctions in
    the building
- bus queues

- lunchtimes
- meals taken
- playgrounds
- trips
- corridors, entrances
    and exits

for evidence of:

- good habits of work and behaviour;
- degrees of self-discipline and mutual support;
- self-confidence and self-esteem;
- attitudes to visitors;
- attitudes to more vulnerable members of community;
- behaviour to non-teaching staff;
- tensions between groups;
- bullying;
- consistency of expectations and appropriate action;
- firm and sensitive staff-pupil discussion;
- ways in which pupils react to school rules and conventions;
- effect of behaviour on the quality of learning.

Inspectors will make these observations at all times. In some cases, they will specifically go to the bus queue or stand at a junction at break. In others, the observation will be part of other observations.

3 Hold discussions with:

- chairperson
- headteacher
- teachers
- pastoral heads
- pupils
- parents
- members of the wider community, eg bus drivers, shopkeepers

for evidence of:

- the promotion of a safe, orderly, co-operative community;
- the promotion of courtesy between all members of the community, including non-teaching members or visitors to it;
- the governors' role in devising a behaviour and discipline policy;
- appropriate strategies to reward good behaviour;
- appropriate strategies to remedy bad behaviour;
- consistency of expectations;
- support to teachers in the management of behaviour;
- partnership/teamwork in implementing behaviour and discipline policy.

Inspectors will hold such conversations during the inspection. These may be part of other conversations or specifically on behaviour.

The Framework has three codicils which are also significant for the school reviewer in this area.

(a) A visitor can influence reactions of pupils in a classroom and a playground (this is also true of the internal reviewer).

(b) The whole-school review and inspection will pull together evidence and judgements in this area from different aspects of the inspection.

(c) Everyone needs to know the statutory basis of the 1986 Education Act and the 1989 Children Act in relation to the forms of punishment which schools may use.

Tracking exercise on behaviour and discipline: zoom lens approach

Sample some pupils. Take two older pupils: one whose behaviour has been good and one whose behaviour required remedial strategies and sanctions. Take two younger pupils who fall into the same categories.

Read their files for evidence of:

– documented rewards
– documented sanctions
– referrals

– teamwork/partnership/ support to teachers
– involvement of parents

Compare the aims of the school's policy with the evidence of the files. Is there evidence in these four sampled histories of Elton's judgement: 'The schools one saw which had positive policies seemed to be very successful in creating an orderly and purposeful atmosphere. They had marginalized bad behaviour by promoting good behaviour'? Discuss with the headteacher, the pastoral head and the class teacher of these sampled children evidence of:

● rewards
● sanctions
● appropriate management

● support to teachers
● school meeting its aims
● school achieving its behaviour policy consistently

Inspectors might look at some children's files during the inspection and track evidence of the management of behaviour.

Structuring an internal review of attendance

A general review: a wide-angle lens

1 Read the documentation, starting with the evaluation criteria set out in

the schedule. Then study the:

- data on attendance by class/year groups/months in year
- data of raw figures (Framework: 'Attendance is to be judged by the levels of pupils' actual attendance')
- data to comply with circular 11/91 – authorized and unauthorized absences
- school's policy/guidance on attendance
- EWO/ESW (Education Welfare Officer/Education Social Worker) records
- data on exclusions
- data on strategies to improve attendance (eg compact, reward system)
- data on strategies to monitor attendance
- information to parents
- data on late arrivals
- data on examination absences

for evidence of:

- extent of attendance (90 per cent OFSTED benchmark);
- extent of non-attendance;
- extent of authorized and unauthorized absence;
- extent of late arrivals;
- evidence of targeted intervention, ie management of pupils whose attendance is a cause of concern;
- meeting legal requirements;
- active system of monitoring attendance and following up absences;
- promotion and maintenance of high attendance rates;
- active system of improving attendance;
- attendance being a school priority;
- communicating to parents school's expectations;
- support to pupils returning to school after period of absence.

Inspectors will look at the data on attendance and at compliance with circular 11/91.

2 Examine the registers for evidence of:

- whole-school consistency
- trends of attendance
- persistent non-attenders
- yearly trends of attendance
- compliance with statutory requirements

Compare a class register with the form register. Conduct a spot check.

After a registration, preferably an afternoon, spot check every teaching class for absences for the whole school. Then compare the list of those absent in classes with the form register and the signing-out book for those who have permission to leave the site. The spot check will also assist in gathering evidence on punctuality to individual lessons.

Such a spot check is not infrequent during an OFSTED inspection. It is a very useful tool for a school reviewer. It can be a regular occurrence in a school to improve the monitoring of attendance and as a statement about the school's prioritization of attendance.

Inspectors will certainly scrutinize registers. They will certainly ask teachers which pupils are absent from the class. A surprise spot check will be carried out in some circumstances.

3 Hold discussions with:

- headteacher   - parents
- pastoral head   - governors
- teachers   - EWO/ESW
- pupils

for evidence of:

- understanding the importance of attendance in the school;
- pupils' enthusiasm to attend;
- pupils' awareness of monitoring;
- governors' awarenesss of their responsibility;
- consistency of approach;
- targeted intervention;
- connection between standards achieved and attendance.

Inspectors will hold such conversations, either specifically or as part of other conversations.

Tracking some cases on attendance: zoom lens approach

Take some samples of children's attendance, say from one class of Year 4 or Year 9 children. Examine the class register, the rewards system given to good attenders, and the files and correspondence with the pupils who are persistent non-attenders for correspondence, referrals and targeted intervention.

Discuss with the class/form teacher and pastoral head the action they have taken to monitor attendance and to target some children to improve attendance. Discuss with them the efficiency of their monitoring and how it fits into the whole-school policy and guidelines. Then make a judgement by the sampled evidence of the extent to which the school's aims, policy and guidelines are being realized in the sampled class(es). Inspectors might undertake this exercise, but it is time-consuming.

Table 7.1 *Pupils' personal development and behaviour*

What School can do for Internal Review		What Inspectors can do	Fwk Ref
For Whole School	For Department/ Curriculum/Area		
Read school aims and departmental schemes for PSMSCD	Departments to trawl documentation for evidence of PSMSCD in curriculum	Read school aims and departmental schemes for PSMSCD	5.1
Look at collective worship (CW) arrangements Legal compliance Record of themes Promote PSMSCD?		Inspect arrangements for CW Legal compliance Record of themes Promote PSMSCD?	5.1
Examine pastoral guidance and code of conduct and community links Match aims and SMSC values		Examine pastoral guidance and code of conduct and community links Match aims and SMSC values	5.1
	Observe PSE lesson on sex education for compliance with governors' policy Match to PSMSCD	Inspect PSE lesson on sex education for compliance with governors' policy	5.1

Table 7.1   continued

What School can do for Internal Review		What Inspectors can do	Fwk Ref
For Whole School	**For Department/ Curriculum/Area**		
Observe collective worship and lessons re delivery of PSMSCD Observe daily life of school and extra-curricular activities	Observe PSE lessons, other lessons and collective worship Observe re delivery of PSMSCD	Inspect PSE lessons re delivery of PSMSCD Inspect collective worship. Observe daily life of school and extra-curricular activities	5.1
Discussions with range of people Evidence of PSMSCD in school		Discussions with range of people Evidence of PSMSCD in school	5.1
	Observe RE lessons for evidence of PSMD	Inspect RE lessons for evidence of PSMD	5.1
Read any written material and noticeboards for evidence of PSMSCD		Read any written material and noticeboards for evidence of PSMSCD	5.1
Read prospectus, behaviour policy and code of conduct Examine for evidence of promotion of good behaviour	See if department's documentation refers to whole-school behaviour policy	Read prospectus, behaviour policy and code of conduct and link to departmental policies Examine for evidence of promotion of good behaviour	5.2

Table 7.1   continued

What School can do for Internal Review		What Inspectors can do	Fwk Ref
For Whole School	**For Department/ Curriculum/Area**		
Examine data on exclusions, referrals and bullying Are expectations consistent, strategic and appropriate?		Examine data on exclusions, referrals and bullying Are expectations consistent, strategic and appropriate?	5.2
Observe lessons for evidence of good habits of behaviour	Observe lessons for evidence of good behaviour	Inspect lessons using grades 1-5 on schedule	5.2
Observe breaktimes, changeovers, bus queues, playgrounds and trips for evidence of good behaviour		Inspect breaktimes, changeover, bus queues, playgrounds and trips for evidence of good behaviour	5.2
Discussions with range of pupils on promotion of safe, orderly community		Discussions with range of pupils on promotion of safe, orderly community	5.2
Sample pupils' files to see match of practice to aims		Sample pupils' files to see match of practice to aims	5.2
Examine attendance data for trends, rates		Inspect attendance data for trends and rates	5.3

Table 7.1   continued

What School can do for Internal Review		What Inspectors can do	Fwk Ref
For Whole School	**For Department/ Curriculum/Area**		
Examine policy on attendance Read data on referrals and exclusions for management of attendance and legal compliance		Examine policy on attendance Read data on referrals and exclusions for management of attendance and legal compliance	5.3
Examine form registers for compliance and management of attendance – spot check	Spot check class registers with form registers	Inspect form registers for compliance and management of attendance – spot check	5.3
Sample some persistent non-attenders' files Match policy to practice		Inspect some persistent non-attenders' files Match policy to practice	5.3
Discussions with range of pupils to match policy to practice	Discuss in department own activities on attendance	Discussions with range of pupils to match policy to practice	5.3

Chapter 8

Management, Administration and Efficiency

(Framework References 6.5 and 4)

'All human life is here' is the slogan of a well-known Sunday newspaper. The same can be said of a school when inspecting its cornerstones: management, administration and efficiency, referred to in this chapter as MAE. No aspect of a school is unaffected by these, and the negative effect, if any of them is deficient, is just as noticeable as the positive effect if all are properly addressed. The Framework rightly says: 'There are few aspects of the work of the school which do not reflect the quality of management'.

Since inspectors are bound by the Framework, due regard must be paid to the four criteria which they will be applying (see Chapter 1, page 18 above). If inspectors find the quality of education or the standards achieved unacceptable, the senior management team will be particularly vulnerable in the areas of management, administration and efficiency. It is wise to review these areas before any inspection. Many schools review them as part of their systematic cycle of review.

Since management, administration and efficiency pervade everything, some schools can be deterred from reviewing them because they simply do not know where to start. In the Framework OFSTED have taken eight key attributes of management and produced a matrix (Part 4, page 65) which makes it possible to collate evidence on management using the Framework headings. A school reviewer could adopt a similar strategy.

A review of management itself needs to be managed carefully; it is a high-risk strategy for headteachers and senior staff. Wise managers, however, know it is vital to a healthy school and they approach it in the same sensitive way in which they handle the review of the quality of teaching and learning. Using criteria, agreeing areas to look at, negotiating methods and shared reporting back will all help to manage it effectively and sensitively.

Some people may think that a review of management applies only to senior management. In fact it needs to involve everyone who has a management responsibility. In the record of evidence, each subject has an evidence form and the management and administration of the subject, aspect or department (7.5) will be evaluated specifically.

In this chapter, all the aspects of management which can be reviewed before an inspection will be covered in detail.

Methods of internal review

There are many ways of structuring an internal review but three in particular have proved very effective.

Structuring an internal review (MAE)

Method 1   'Pupil pursuit'

'Pupil pursuit' has traditionally been used to review the quality of the learning experience for a child on a daily basis. It is a commonly used method, too, for examining the quality of the curriculum in one class. It is, however, also a most effective way of asking: how does the management and planning of a school affect the learning opportunities for this child; how does the organization and efficiency of the school support his or her learning? Is the school's leadership effective in achieving the desired outcome? For example, if a school reviewer is 'pursuing' a pupil, all the questions below can be asked in a single lesson:

– Is the organization of the day helpful to the pupil?
– Did the lesson start and finish on time?
– Is the teacher in control of the environment?

- Has the environment been organized attractively, in a stimulating way for learning and appropriately for this lesson?
- Is the teacher clear where the lesson fits into the programme of study and the scheme of work?
- Does the planning and organization of this lesson reflect departmental planning and the demands of the National Curriculum?
- What departmental guidance has the teacher received?
- Are the resources appropriate, adequate, accessible and helpful?
- Where appropriate, is the charging policy in use?
- Is there evidence of any earmarked funding?
- Is there assessment and recording here?
- Is behaviour well managed in this lesson?
- Is attendance checked? Is there a system? Does the system feed into a school system?
- Do the children have a homework diary? Is it used efficiently?
- What monitoring and evaluation procedures are there to moderate the standards of achievement?
- Is the atmosphere purposeful and businesslike? Does the atmosphere in this lesson reflect the school's atmosphere?
- Does the timetable reflect accurately this lesson?
- What information does the display noticeboard give?
- Is IT used in any way for the lesson (curriculum, organization or administration)?
- When appropriate, is cover being managed well and efficiently?
- What monitoring and evaluation procedures are there to moderate the quality of learning and teaching?
- Is the equal opportunities policy being well managed? How?
- How is SEN managed, planned and organized?
- Is the lesson being taught in a specialist room?
- Is the accommodation and furniture appropriate and well-managed?
- Is there provision for support staff, and how is this managed?
- Do the pupils know how to find and use resources?
- Is everyone punctual to the lesson? What system is there for late arrivals?
- Is it an orderly lesson?
- Is everyone prepared for work?
- How well does the teacher use his or her time and expertise?
- Are the relationships in this class good?

Method 2 Interviews with core questions

It is very helpful to take the school development plan as a starting point. It can be used to review the school by asking a variety of people the same penetrating questions. The method consists of interviewing as many of the following as possible to discuss with them the questions set out below:

- chairperson
- headteacher
- deputy heads/senior teachers
- some heads of department/ subject postholders
- some pastoral heads/postholders with key stage responsibility

- some teachers
- secretarial staff
- another governor, preferably a parent
- finance officer

The core questions are given below but reviewers can modify them for each person. For example, question 7 would not be appropriate for governors, whereas, for example, question 12 would be put as it stands for a head of department, for the chairperson and the headteacher. It could be framed for the individual teacher as 'Do you know how your departmental allowance is decided upon? Does your department have any way of monitoring and evaluating the educational outcome of your financial allowance?' For the finance officer: 'How do you control the departmental expenditure?'

Core questions

1 What part did you play in the construction of last year's school development plan (SDP)?
2 What part did you play in evaluating last year's SDP?
3 What part did you play in the construction of this year's SDP?
4 How does this year's SDP set targets? Does planning look beyond the next school or financial year?
5 Does your department/area/year team have its own plan/target?
6 How do they (5) fit into this year's SDP?
7 Do you have a job description? Who is your line manager? How are you accountable to them? How are tasks delegated to you?
8 What is your role in managing and planning for the area(s) for which you are responsible?

9 (a) What is your role in monitoring and evaluating in the area(s) for which you are responsible?

(b) Are you involved in evaluating the cost effectiveness of an area, provision, or many areas? How?

10 How do you communicate with others in the school and with parents?

11 What team-building strategies do you use to achieve these targets?

12 How is the departmental allowance decided upon? How is it controlled? How is it evaluated for effective educational outcome? How is it linked to the SDP?

13 Do you have access to earmarked funds or any other monies?

14 Who decides, and how, on the school's expenditure policy? How are funds allocated to budget heads? How involved are the governors in managing resources?

15 What is the school's charging policy? How does this affect you?

16 What is the school's pay policy? (How does this affect you?)

17 What are the control systems of expenditure?

18 Do you consider that the school runs efficiently? Why/Why not? What are the key points for action in relation to efficiency?

19 How does the rooming policy affect you?

20 Do you have easy access to the senior management team?

21 What is your involvement in whole-school decision making? How are whole-school policies formulated?

22 What review of resources do you oversee?

23 By what criteria do you decide on INSET provision?

24 How are the SDP's targets matched to financial allocations? Is there evidence of an educational rationale in budget planning?

25 How are the SDP's targets matched to INSET?

26 Who makes the decisions for staff deployment, groupings and roomings?

27 What system of moderation of standards of achievement do you use in the department and school?

28 How does the governing body/SMT/headteacher give the school direction, purpose and vision?

29 How is this communicated to pupils, staff and parents?

30 What are the school's aims? How do you realize them in your area of responsibility?

31 What meetings do you attend? How regular, frequent and efficient are they?

32 Do meetings which you attend make decisions, engage in consultation and initiate consultation?

33 How does the governing body operate with its sub-committees? How does this affect you?

34 Has the governing body completed the questionnaire, 'Keeping Your Balance'? (issued by Audit Commission in August 1993.)

35 What steps has the school taken in response to the most recent auditors' report?

36 What criteria do you use to evaluate achievement? Do you use any value added measures?

When the reviewer has asked a wide range of people these questions (or modified versions of these questions), the reviewer will be able to check for consistency, both from the interviewees and from the relevant documentation. The reviewer will then be able to form a view of the management, planning, organisation and efficiency, and if necesary put remedial measures in hand before an inspection.

Method 3 Using a matrix

The third method is a more mechanistic one and involves taking the Framework as the precise structure for internal review. The reviewer draws up a matrix using the evaluation criteria from the Framework (white pages for evaluation criteria and blue pages for the amplification of evaluation criteria) on one axis, and on the other axis, the area to be reviewed. See Table 8.1.*

Table 8.1 *Matrix for evaluating MAE*

	Evaluation Criteria MAE	Science	ARR	Attendance	Behaviour	PSMSCD	EO
7.5	Targets set						
	Policy in place						
	Action plan for targets						
	Responsiblity delegated						

Table 8.1 continued

	Evaluation Criteria MAE	Science	ARR	Attendance	Behaviour	PSMSCD	EO
	Evaluation of targets						
	Place in SDP						
	Costs assessed						
	Training needs						
	Efficiency of routine admin.						
	Communication of information						
	Use of IT						
	Well-planned daily routine/ clear respon-sibilities						
4	Time linked to targets						
	Money linked to targets						
	Staff linked to targets						
	Resources linked to educational outcome						

* On the horizontal axis ARR = Assessment, Recording and Reporting, PSMSCD = Pupils' Spiritual, Moral, Social and Cultural Development, and EO = Equal Opportunities

Some reviewers will want to write descriptive judgements against the matrix. Others may want to use OFSTED's grading system, which is certainly quicker and more mechanistic in approach. Whether the judgement is descriptive or numerical, the reviewer will need to be clear about the basis of the judgement and the evidence for it.

The three models provide three different approaches to reviewing MAE internally. In all three models the reviewer is trying to build up a picture like that shown in Figure 8.1.

Figure 8.1

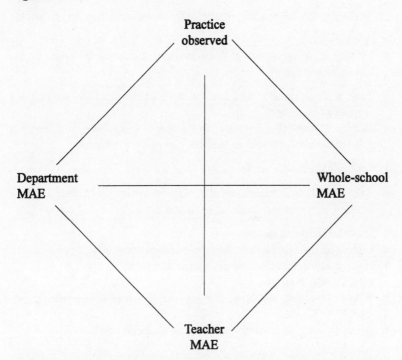

Something needs to be said, too, about the governing body. The inspectors will inspect a school. Reviewers will review the school. In reviewing or inspecting the school, the direction of the governing body, its leadership, its involvement, its commitment and relationship with the school will be included. The Framework places the governing body centrally and is very explicit, for example, about the governors' responsibilities for budget management. This is a very sensitive issue for school reviewers. It might provide one of many reasons why a governor should be involved in the school review process.

Review of evidence and criteria

Management and Administration – 7.5

Let us now look at how to examine the evidence:

1 Trawl through the school prospectus for aims, objectives and policies.

- Are they clear?
- Do they cover all aspects of the school, and are they appropriate for the full range of pupils?

2 Take a subject policy and see if it reflects the aims, objectives, and policies of the school prospectus.

3 Take a whole-school policy, for example behaviour, and see if it reflects the aims, objectives, and policies of the prospectus.

- Where is the match or mismatch?

4 Take the school development plan. The full review in Method 2 can be adopted, or a more streamlined approach.

- Link the budget to targets.
- Link departmental plans to the whole-school development plan.
- Is there any monitoring and evaluation of targets?
- Link INSET to targets.
- Who is involved, and how, in the cycle of school development planning?
- Does planning go beyond this school or financial year?

5 Take a selection of minutes and agendas, including governors' meetings and working parties. Ask for the meetings calendar and examine it.

- Is there evidence of decisions involving a variety of groups?
- Is there evidence of overall management and planning through a wide set of constituencies?
- Is there a decision which can be tracked through meetings/SDP/working parties? Who is consulted?

- What are the roles of the SMT and the governors in decision-making?
- From whom do ideas start?
- Are governors well-informed about their responsibilities?
- Are agendas and minutes (including those of the GB) available?
- Do minutes clearly distinguish between consultative items and decisions made?
- Do meetings have clear remits?
- Do meetings appear efficient from the minutes?

6 Look at the latest budget outturn statement and monthly profile, showing planned and actual spending against each budget head. (See also pages 136–7 below.)

- Is there evidence that the budget has been planned?
- Is there evidence that the budget heads reflect the SDP targets?
- What policies are there for budget allocations? Are they followed?

7 Set up interviews with a cross-section of staff and governors to gather evidence:

- Headteacher
- Senior managers
- Head of department
- Pastoral head
- A teacher
- Member of non-teaching staff
- Parent governor
- Pupil (for some questions)

Ask them questions, for example:

- What is your job description?
- Who is your line manager?
- How are you accountable?
- How are tasks delegated to you?
- What INSET and professional development are planned for you?
- How are you involved in planning and development within the school?
- What new initiatives would you draw attention to?
- What do you think the strengths of the school are?
- What do you think the weaknesses of the school are?
- Have the governors fulfilled their statutory responsibilities with regard to sex education and collective worship?
- What monitoring and evaluating roles do you fulfil in the area(s) for which you are responsible?
- Do all staff have job descriptions? Are these working documents?

- What targets have been set for your area(s) this year? Is the time-scale reasonable?
- How is the curriculum managed through the middle manager?
- What is the evidence for the management, evaluation and monitoring of one aspect of school life, for example attendance? How are governors involved in this aspect?

8 Examine the pupils', parents' and staff handbooks for:

- clear and appropriate language
- efficiency
- comprehensiveness
- consistency
- unobtrusive systems

Is the staff handbook developmental? Have you made yourself a hostage to the rhetoric? Does practice observed match the rhetoric? How does the school ensure that the roles and responsibilities of all staff are communicated to each other?

9 Examine noticeboards for:

- clarity
- efficiency
- attractiveness
- usefulness

Check positive and negative aspects.
10 Is there a briefing of staff?

- How?
- When?
- Is it useful?
  Evidence of?

11 Is there a briefing of pupils/parents or newsletter/news items in assembly? Are these:

- clear
- efficient
- useful
- is the language appropriate for non-English speakers?

12 Examine the daily routine:

- 'pupil pursuit'
- attend registration
- attend assemblies
- observe lunch
- walk the school at breaks/lunchtime
- walk the school at the start and end of the day
- stand with the bus queues
- check duties
- stand in junctions at lesson change

13 Take one aspect of the school, for example attendance. Ask how it is organized and administered. Is it done:

- efficiently?
- effectively?
- is IT used?
- is there a well-planned routine?
- are people's duties and responsibilities clear at all levels?
- is it unobtrusive in its administration?
- what routine spot checks are made?

14 Take the calendar of the school year as a major piece of evidence:

- is it efficiently constructed?
- is it clear and helpful?
- how are amendments made?
- how is it communicated and to whom?
- how does the calendar of meetings fit into it?
- can consultation work within the cycle of meetings?

15 Timetable. An examination of the timetable will come into many aspects of school review. From the focus of administration, questions such as the following should be rigorously asked:

- Is it clear?
- Are amendments published?
- Does it communicate to staff and pupils what it needs to?
- Does it appear in good time for planning by departments/class teachers?

16 Assessment, Recording, Reporting and the mechanics

- Do they fit into national requirements?
- Do departmental/year procedures fit into school requirements?
- Are these mechanics efficient, clear and effective?
- Is communication with pupils and parents clear and effective?
- Have you asked a pupil or a parent what they think?

17 Discipline arrangements
This is thoroughly reviewed elsewhere (see Chapter 7, pages 115–17). Here it is used as evidence of a well-managed and administered school.

- What are the discipline arrangements?
- Are they clearly communicated to all parents, pupils and staff?

- What evidence is there of their effectiveness?
- What is the time cost to staff of these arrangements?

18 Staff cover for absence

- Who manages it?
- Is it efficient? Evidence?
- What is the cost?

19 IT in administration

- Where is IT used for school administration?
- Where could it be used?
- Is it efficiently used?

Review of evidence of efficiency – 4

There is inevitably much overlap between Efficiency (4) and Management and Administration (7.5). When undertaking a school review and talking with a head of department about their part in the process of school development planning, the reviewer should ask questions about the financial implications of the SDP in the department. He or she should:

1 Examine the SDP for the relationships between targets and the allocation of the budget. Then examine the evaluation part of the SDP in terms of educational outcome against the budgets spent.
2 Examine departmental plans/targets and their relationship to the allocation of resources and the evaluation of outcome against resources. Who is involved in decision-making?
3 Review (with a governor and the finance officer) the:

- allocation of resources
- control systems of all money
- details of additional income
- charging policies
- allocation to budget heads
- who is involved in these processes?

4 Review current budget profile and the most recent annual out-turn statement of expenditure against budget.
5 Reviewers may want to prepare unit cost and unit expenditure on books, materials and equipment and compare them to the SDP targets.
6 Senior managers can collect all the data and (a) review staffing costs by year and subject, and (b) review all allocation of allowances for staff by department, gender, pastoral/academic areas and grade. They

can also examine teaching staff and non-teaching staff costs as percentage of budget. (See also pupil – teacher ratio in Chapter 5, page 78.) Note that a new pay structure took effect from September 1993.

7   Review and analyse:

- room use
- specialist match

- percentage usage
- who decides on room allocation and how?

Note that the DfE is producing a new method of analysing space use for the curriculum.

8   Review the allocation of resources to:

- internal decoration
- IT equipment
- furniture

- refurbishment
- A/V materials

9   What are the priorities in the organization of directed time?

Table 8.2   *Efficiency, management and administration*

What School can do for Internal Review		What Inspectors can do	Fwk Ref
For Whole School	**For Department/ Curriculum/Area**		
Read staff handbook, pupils' handbook, parents' handbook and prospectus for: clarity efficiency consistency aims/objectives policies language	Do departmental policies reflect school aims? Do departmental policies match whole-school policies eg: charging EO SEN	Inspect staff handbook, pupils' handbook, parents' handbook and prospectus for clarity etc Inspect departmental policies and compare match with above documents and whole-school policies Match policies to practice	7.5

Table 8.2   continued

What School can do for Internal Review		What Inspectors can do	Fwk Ref
For Whole School	**For Department/ Curriculum/Area**		
Read a whole-school policy Examine whether it reflects the prospectus		Inspect whole-school policy and see if it reflects the prospectus	7.5
Review of SDP: processes who is involved and how	Review of involvement in SDP and departmental development plan	Inspect SDP Ask questions about consultation/processes of construction Compare SDP and departmental development plans Interviews	7.5
Review SDP targets Match to budget allocations and monitoring and evaluation of educational outcome	Examine departmental development plans and match them and SDP to our finances and monitoring and evaluation of educational outcome	Inspect relationship between targets and budgetary allocations of SDP and departments and evaluation of educational outcome	7.5
Review SDP and links to INSET	Review SDP and departmental development plans and links to INSET	Inspect SDP and departmental development plans and links to INSET Interviews	7.5

Table 8.2   continued

What School can do for Internal Review		What Inspectors can do	Fwk Ref
For Whole School	**For Department/ Curriculum/Area**		
Sample minutes and agendas of wide range of meetings Review decision-making	Review departmental minutes and agendas Review decision-making with department and the way the department fits into school decision-making	Inspect minutes and agendas Inspect decision-making in school, areas, departments and working parties Track a decision Attend meetings Interviews	7.5
Review allocations to budget headings Review how these reflect SDP targets Monitor action on completed questionnaire 'Keeping your Balance'		Inspect budget out-turn statement and monthly profiles Analyse previous over and under spends Make comparisons with budgets of similar schools Inspect policies of allocation of and relationship between budget heads and targets in SDP Inspect latest audit report Inspect evidence of planning and flexibility in response to change	7.5

Table 8.2   continued

What School can do for Internal Review		What Inspectors can do	Fwk Ref
For Whole School	**For Department/ Curriculum/Area**		
		Inspect questionnaire 'Keeping your Balance' Interview wide range of people	
Review job descriptions for complete school, and working documents Review line management accountability and delegation	Review job descriptions for complete department, and working documents Review line management	Interviews with wide range of staff on job descriptions, line management, accountability and delegation	7.5
Review evaluation and monitoring as management function Take SDP Take one aspect Look at cycle of review Look at value added measures	Review evaluation and monitoring as middle management function Departmental development plan Meetings Moderation Classroom observation Double marking Review value added measures	Inspect evaluation and monitoring throughout school SDP Interviews Practice observed in classroom Inspect value added measures	7.5

Table 8.2 continued

What School can do for Internal Review		What Inspectors can do	Fwk Ref
For Whole School	**For Department/ Curriculum/Area**		
Review school noticeboards for: clarity efficiency attractiveness usefulness	Review departmental noticeboards for: clarity efficiency attractiveness usefulness	Inspect noticeboards	7.5
Review briefing for staff, pupils, newsletters and communications home for: clarity efficiency attractiveness language	Review communications from this department for: clarity efficiency attractiveness language	Inspect all methods of communication, oral and written, to staff, pupils and parents Attend briefing Attend a parents' evening Attend assembly	7.5
Review routines for efficiency and unobtrusiveness, eg: buses duty tutorials registration breaks lunch ends/starts assemblies	Review routines, eg: new books new exercise books reports	Inspect routines Buses duty Staff duty Attend registration Attend assemblies Breaks – stand at junctions Observe lesson changes Attend briefing Pursue pupil/class	7.5

Table 8.2   continued

What School can do for Internal Review		What Inspectors can do	Fwk Ref
For Whole School	For Department/ Curriculum/Area		
		Eat lunch with pupils Stand in entrance hall at start of day	
Take one aspect, eg attendance Review registers with EWO/ESW across school Review flow chart of action on absence Review by tracking one absentee Review lates Conduct spot check	Is there class registration? (Secondary only) What is relationship between that and tutorial register?	Inspect registers (if time) Interview pastoral heads Interview EWO/ESW Interview pupil Spot check all classes for one lesson in the week	7.5
Review calendar for: construction efficiency amendments distribution meetings cycle	Place in meetings cycle Contribution to effect of school calendar	Inspect calendar Inspect meetings calendar Track a decision through cycle of meetings Attend meeting Interviews	7.5

Table 8.2 continued

What School can do for Internal Review		What Inspectors can do	Fwk Ref
For Whole School	**For Department/ Curriculum/Area**		
Review timetable for: clarity publication date amendments effective communication	Role in writing timetable	Inspect it Talk to HOD, timetabler and teacher	7.5
Review ARR for: compliance efficiency workability effectiveness communication to parents	Review part in ARR for whole school Review department for: compliance efficiency effectiveness	Inspect procedures Interview DH Interview HOD Interview parent(s) Interview pupil	7.5
Review discipline arrangements for: organization clear rules clear communication effectiveness How does reviewer know?	Role of department in discipline	Inspect documentation Interview pastoral heads Interview teachers Interview DH Interview parent governor Observe practice	7.5 5.2

Table 8.2   continued

What School can do for Internal Review		What Inspectors can do	Fwk Ref
For Whole School	**For Department/ Curriculum/Area**		
Review staff cover for efficiency and effectiveness of system, and cost to school	Review How does it affect the department? How does the department affect it?	Inspect documentation Observe cover being done at start of day Interview person in charge Is it done effectively and efficiently?	7.5
Review IT in administration	Review departmental benefits from IT in administration	Observe its use in practice Inspect documentation	7.5
Review methods of allocation of resources/control system Use governors' finance sub-committee minutes	Review budget allocation/control system	Interview governors Read auditors' reports Inspect budget statements/financial policies Inspect control systems	4
Review current budget profile and most recent annual out-turn statement		Interview finance officers Interview HOD	4
Prepare unit costs and unit expenditure on books etc	Prepare unit costs	Inspect unit costs	4 7.6 (ii)
Analyse staff costs	(Analyse staff costs)	Inspect staff costs	4 7.6 (i)
Analyse room use	Analyse room use	Inspect room use	4

Postscript: 20 Things to Consider for Review and Preparation for Inspection

1 Review whole-school documentation

- Prospectus
- Aims and objectives/mission statement
- Curriculum statement
- School development plan
- Staff handbook
- Assessment policy and guidelines
- Behaviour and discipline policy
- Arrangements for pupils' welfare and guidance
- Equal opportunities policy
- Special educational needs policy
- Whole curriculum and cross-curricular provision
- Attendance policy and documentation
- Extra-curricular provision
- Spiritual, moral, social and cultural development
- Use of the library and learning resources
- Governors' policies generally.

Note that all documentation will be scrutinized before an inspection begins and a pre-inspection commentary written on its quality, together with issues to be followed up, such as the match betwen policy and practice.

2 Review curriculum documentation and planning

- Match with whole-school policies, such as special needs, equal opportunities, cross-curricular provision
- Schemes of work
- Curriculum organization and planning
- Assessment, recording and reporting
- Teaching and learning strategies
- Use of resources
- Development plan for the curriculum area
- Use of non-teaching staff.

3 Examine the quality and range of the curriculum

- Curriculum plans and timetables
- Implementation of the National Curriculum and basic curriculum
- Arrangement and composition of teaching groups
- Cross-curricular themes, dimensions and skills
- Nature and support for extra-curricular activities
- Pre-vocational education including careers education and work experience
- Personal and social education.

4 Review provision for pupils with special educational needs

- Whole-school policy and procedures
- Staffing provision and expertise including use of school support teachers
- Extent and appropriateness of integration
- Differentiated teaching
- Specialist accommodation and resources
- Pupil groupings
- Arrangements for monitoring funding for pupils with SEN.

5 Review assessment procedures

- Assessment policy, guidelines and procedures
- Procedures for reviewing and monitoring the progress of individual pupils
- Records of pupils' achievement and arrangements for reporting to parents
- Analysis of National Curriculum assessments and external examinations and any other assessment data in order to improve pupils' performance
- Samples of pupils' work.

6 Work with staff on the quality of teaching, quality of learning and standards of achievement criteria

- Lesson observation pro forma
- Grading
- Criteria for assessment
- Evidence.

7 Examine equality of opportunity

- Policy statements
- Classroom organization and management, teaching and differentiation
- Curriculum content and access
- Needs arising from gender, ability, ethnicity and social circumstance
- Appropriateness of resources
- Standards of achievement of individuals and groups.

8 Review pupils' moral, spiritual, social and cultural development

- Quality of relationships in the school
- Values, beliefs and attitudes which the school promotes and demonstrates

- Policy and procedures relating to attendance and punctuality
- Code of conduct, rewards and sanctions
- Procedures for monitoring exclusions and referrals (including bullying)
- Extent and range of pupils' social and cultural activities
- The range of, and pupils' reponses to, opportunities for extensive responsibility and initiative.

9 Review pupils' welfare and guidance

- Pastoral care and guidance systems
- Child protection policy and procedures
- Health education programme and sex education policy
- Procedures for assuring pupils' well-being, health and safety
- Use made of specialist services.

10 Examine staffing issues

- Staffing policy (including use of financial incentives)
- Job descriptions
- Staff development policy
- INSET records (last three years)
- Match of qualifications and teaching
- NQT induction
- Arrangements for appraisal
- Use of non-teaching staff.

11 Review management, organization and administration

- School development planning
- Policies for making budget allocations
- Organization of meetings
- Daily routine of administration and organization of the school
- Communications both internal and external
- Establishment of effective working relationships
- Means of promoting quality and planning improvement.

12 Examine the management of resources for learning

- Library provision
- Information technology resources
- Use made of funds raised by the school or through sponsorship
- Unit cost and unit expenditure on books, material and equipment in comparison with local and national levels
- Use of out-of-school resources, such as residential facilities and education visits
- Access to specialist resources for pupils with SEN.

13 Examine the efficiency of the school

- Procedures, systems and working practices on the quality of planning
- School budget profile
- Arrangements for monitoring the budget and making financial decisions
- Management and use of accommodation and resources for learning
- System for communicating information
- Use made of information technology in school management and administration.

14 Review the school accommodation

- Teaching areas, use of specialized accommodation
- Reception areas
- Library
- Common areas
- Display/exhibitions
- Grounds
- Use of buildings/accessibility.

15 Review standards of achievement

- Pupils' competence in literacy, oracy and numeracy

- Results of national assessments and examinations
- Records of progress and achievement
- Evidence of value added.

16 Establish levels of legal compliance

- National Curriculum
- Reporting to parents
- RE
- Collective worship
- Attendance procedures
- Health and safety.

17 Evaluate links with parents, the community and other agencies

- Information and communication systems to parents
- Contribution to school life
- Relationships with business and commerce, LEAs and other relevant agencies
- Effective use of work experience
- Quality of liaison arrangements with other schools and institutions.

18 Involve governors

- In policy development
- In monitoring and review
- Responsibilities to be inspected
- School development and budget planning.

19 Study the inspection schedule with reference to

- Evaluation criteria
- Evidence

- What the report will include
- Quality gaps.

20 Review monitoring and evaluation systems

- Action planning and success criteria
- Line management systems
- Team development plans
- Curriculum reviews
- Classroom observation
- Assessment checks
- Evaluation of quality and standards.

Note that a crucial question that will be posed to all senior management teams will be: 'How do you review/inspect your own school?' This is worth summing up in a strategy document.

Bibliography

DES (1989) *School Indicators for Internal Management: an aide-memoire,* DES.

DFE, Circular 7/93, *Inspecting Schools: A Guide to the Inspection Provisions of the Educational (Schools) Act 1992 in England.*

Gray, John (1990) 'The Quality of School: Frameworks for Judgement', *British Journal of Education Studies,* XXXVIII, pp 204–23.

HMI (1988) *Secondary Schools: An Appraisal by HMI,* HMSO.

HMI (1992; 2nd edn, 1993) *Handbook for the Inspection of Schools,* HMSO.

HMSO (1992) *The Education (Schools) Act,* HMSO.

Mortimore, P., Sammons, P. *et al.* (1988) *School Matters – The Junior Years,* Open Books.

Rutter, M. *et al.* (1979) *Fifteen Thousand Hours, Secondary Schools and their Effects on Children,* Open Books.

Smith, D. and Tomlinson, S. (1989) *The School Effect – A Study of Multiracial Comprehensives,* Policy Studies Institute.

Tizard, B., Blatchford, P *et al.* (1988) *Young Children at School in the Inner City,* Laurence Erlbaum.

INDEX

A Levels 57
academic progress 17
action planning 32, 37, 47–8
activity observation, proforma for 84
added value *see* value added
administration *see* management, administration and efficiency
agencies, links with 150
ALIS (A Level Information System) 57, 71
assessment procedures 147
attendance *see* pupils' personal development and behaviour

change processes 19
Children Act 1989 36
classroom observation 71–3
community, links with 150
comprehensive schools, multi-racial 15–16
curriculum
  checklist for whole-school review 88
  classroom planning and delivery reviewing 101–2
  consistency 87
  content, organization and planning 85–8
  cross-curricular checklist for review 91–2
cross-curricular themes, skills and dimensions 89–92
  documentation 85–6, 88, 99–101, 146
  equality of opportunity 92–4
    checklist for review 93–4
  extra-curricular activities 98–9
  methods of reviewing quality and range 99–102
  objectives 87
  personal and social education 96–7
  planning 146
  pre-vocational 97–8
  quality and range of 146
  special education needs (SEN) 94–6
    checklist for review 95–6
  subject/reviewing for consistent documentation 100–101
  whole-school curriculum documentation audit 99–100
curriculum and curriculum provisions 23–4

development-planning 19
documentation
  curriculum 85–6, 88, 99–101, 146
  review whole-school 145
  school review 43–4

Education Reform Act 1988 17, 86, 89

Education (Schools) Act 1992 18, 22

effective schools *see* school effectiveness

efficiency *see* management, administration and efficiency

equality of opportunity 92–4, 147
  checklist for review 93–4

evaluation systems 17

extra-curricular activities 98–9

Framework for Inspection 22–4, 70–71, 124, 129

GCSE 57

GEST (Grant for Education, Support and Training) 51, 71

governing bodies
  after inspection 32
  before inspection 31–2
  checklist of roles and responsibilities during inspections 33
  during inspection 32
  involvement of 150
  responsibilities in relation to inspection 31
  role in monitoring and evaluation 49
  role in school review 45, 51

guidelines for review and internal development in schools (GRIDS) 19

Handbook for the Inspection of Schools 10, 18, 25, 33

headteachers and staff
  after inspection 34
  before inspection 33–4
  checklist for inspections 34–5
  during inspection 34

Her Majesty's Chief Inspectors of Schools (HMCI) 22, 24, 27, 28

improvement programmes 20

infant schools 16

inspection process 22–38, 23–4
  after inspection 38
  before inspection 38
  content, evaluation criteria and evidence base 23–4
  duration of 23
  during inspection 38
  function of 22
  governing bodies' role in 31–3
  heads' and staff role in 33–4
  management of 20
  methodology 25
  new procedures 22
  parents' role in 36–7
  provision for 22
  pupils' role in 35–6
  purpose of 10
  quality and reliability of 22
  record of evidence 24
  schedule 150
  special measures 26–7
  summary of items to consider 145–51
  see also Framework for Inspectors; Lay Inspectors; Registered Inspectors

inspection report 25–6, 37
inspection teams 23, 29–30
  checklist of duties 30

junior schools, key factors of
  effectiveness 16

Keeping the School under Review 8

lay inspectors 23, 29, 30–31
  assignments of 30
  purpose of 30
learning quality 69–84, 147
  grade definitions 69
LEAs 20, 26, 32
legal compliance 150
lesson observation 41–2, 58–61, 70
  proforma for 83
Local Management of Schools 17

management, administration and
  efficiency 124–44, 148
  interviews with core questions
    127–9
  key attributes 124
  matrix evaluation 129–32
  methods of internal review 125
  review of evidence and criteria
    efficiency 136–7
  management and
    administration 132–6
  review process 124–5
  structuring an internal review
    125–32
matrix for evaluating MAE
  129–32
monitoring and evaluation 17–18,
  48–9, 55

reviewing 151

National Curriculum 29, 54–6, 87,
  94, 96

observation of activities 42
observation schedule 69
Office for Standards in Education
  see OFSTED
OFSTED 8, 10, 20, 23, 25–9,
  31–3, 41, 51, 52, 57, 58, 69, 86,
  92, 124

parents
  links with 150
  role in inspection process 36–7
  role in school review 45
performance indicators 17
performance monitoring 17–18
personal education 96–7
Pre-Inspection Content and School
  Indicator (PICSI) 57
primary schools 14
  value added 57–8
process factors and characteristics
  14, 18–19
process indicators 19
pupil profiles, standards of
  achievement 62
'pupil pursuit' 42–3, 125–6
pupil–teacher relationships 18
pupils
  case studies in school review
    46
  moral, spiritual, social and
    cultural development 147–8
  personal development and
    behaviour 109–23

difficulties for school
reviewer 109
output judgements 109
structuring internal review
114–15
attendance 117–20
behaviour and discipline
115–17
tracking cases on attendance
119–20
tracking exercise on behaviour
and discipline 117
role during inspection 35–6
role in school review 45
sampling of work 74
satisfaction 18
social and academic progress 13
spiritual, moral, social and
cultural development,
method of internal review
110–13
spiritual, moral, social and
cultural development
(PSMSCD) 109, 110
tracking a sample of 114–15
standards of achievement 61–2
welfare and guidance 148

quality achieved *see* standards of
achievement
quality concerns 13–21
quality indicators 17

Race Relations Act 1976 92
records of achievement 62
Registered Inspectors 23, 24,
26–9, 32, 36, 37
checklist of duties 29

requirements of 28
resource management 149
sampling of pupils 46
sampling of work 44
sampling pupils' work 74
scheme of work 102
school accommodation 149
school development planning 18,
40, 50
school effectiveness
areas of concern 14
characteristics of 21
criteria for 15, 19
external judgement on 11
indicators of 17
'internal' inspection and review
of 10
international research 16–17
key factors in 14–15
major studies of 14–17
research 13–20
variation over time 14
variation within schools 13–14
school improvement
concern for 13–21
criteria and processes for 13–21
school review 39–51
achieving future goals 47
challenges of 49–51
checklist of questions for 55–6
cycle of 40
documentation 43–4
ensuring rigour 41
formulating future goals 46–7
gathering evidence 41–6, 49
governors' role 45, 51
link to external inspection 41
methodology 41–9

monitoring and evaluation 48–9
parents' views 45
processes of 39–40
pupils' views 45
purpose of 10
sampling of pupils 46
sampling of work 44
spot check 46
summary of items to consider 145–51
targets 49
teachers' views 44
time problem 49–50
see also pupils, personal development and behaviour
Secondary Schools: An Appraisal by HMI 15
secondary schools
criteria for effectiveness 15
inspections 29
Sex Discrimination Act 1975 92
social education 96–7
special education needs (SEN) 30, 53
checklist for review 95–6
curriculum 94–6
provision for pupils with 146
special measures, schools requiring 26–7
special schools 53
staffing issues 148
standards of achievement 52–68, 147
analysis of data 54–6
assessing 53–4
grades for 69
high 52

lesson observation 58–61
low 52–3
pupils' profiles 62
pupils' work 61–2
reviewing 149–50
subject areas 56
subject/learning area 63–4
whole-school strategies for reviewing 62–3

teachers
involvement of 19–20
views in school review 44
teaching quality 69–84, 147
classroom observation 71–3
evaluation criteria 70
external observers 70
grade definitions 69
methods of internal review 71–5
review of evidence and criteria 75–8
sampling pupils' work 74
transect 46, 75
Training and Enterprise Council (TEC) 31
transect 46, 75

value added 56–8, 71
primary schools 57–8
statistical treatment 57

YELLIS (Year 11 Information System) 57, 71
Young Children at School in the Inner City 16